D0590337

THE MINDFULNESS BOOK

PRACTICAL WAYS TO LEAD A MORE MINDFUL LIFE

MARTYN NEWMAN

LONDON   NEW YORK   BOGOTA
MADRID   BARCELONA   BUENOS AIRES
MEXICO CITY   MONTERREY   SAN FRANCISCO
SHANGHAI

Published by
LID Publishing Ltd
One Adam Street
London
WC2N 6LE
United Kingdom

31 West 34th Street, Suite 8004,
New York, NY 1001, US

info@lidpublishing.com
www.lidpublishing.com

A member of:

www.businesspublishersroundtable.com

Printed in the Czech Republic by Finidr

ISBN: 978-1-910649-63-3

Cover and page design: Caroline Li
Illustration: Sara Taheri

CONTENTS

ACKNOWLEDGEMENTS

This book represents more than a decade of experience teaching mindfulness to private and corporate clients around the world.

I am indebted to many who have contributed to my thinking and practise, but especially to Dr B. Alan Wallace, one of the world's leading authorities on the practise of mindfulness. Alan is a friend and colleague, but above all my teacher and mentor in the practise of mindfulness and meditation. Although I have integrated Western psychological perspectives and methods into the strategies described in this book, many of the practices have their origins in the training I undertook with Alan.

This book would not have come together if not for Sara Taheri and Niki Mullin, from LID Publishing, who first approached me to write the book. I am grateful to them for their confidence in the project and patience in seeing it through to completion.

Thanks to the team at RocheMartin for their support throughout the project. Judy Purse, Geraldine Abberton, Bev Stansfield and Bea Lynch all took on extra work to shield me from the demands of a growing business and freed up my time to write.

Finally, special thanks to my partner, Suzy Turkovic, for her loving support of both me and, particularly, our young son, Sebastian, through the many early mornings and long weekends dedicated to writing.

Sebastian James Newman, this one's for you.

INTRODUCTION

The faculty of voluntarily bringing back a wandering attention over and over again is the very root of judgment, character and will. . . . An education which should improve this faculty would be the education par excellence.

William James, *Principles of Psychology*, 1890

Near the turn of the 20th century, the celebrated Harvard professor and my favorite psychologist, William James, made a startling observation. He noticed that the ability to focus our minds by bringing our attention back to the present moment was the indispensible skill that enabled people to take control of their lives and achieve their potential.

Okay, hardly a discovery worthy of a Nobel Prize. And you don't need to be an air-traffic controller to know that some activities just need absolute presence of mind to lead to better outcomes. But more than a century later, that simple observation has had a profoundly positive impact on the lives of millions of people.

According to James, the ability to bring your attention back to the present moment repeatedly leads to "better judgment, character and willpower". And, he cautions, if you lack this ability, then you cannot say you are the "master of yourself". He went on to insist that the best education would be one that helps to improve this ability.

Now that's something we can all agree on. Think how often during the day you find yourself tired, stressed and irritable, your only refuge being momentary daydreaming about the past or future. Anxious thoughts pinball in your head, making it near impossible to power down and relax. For many people, this condition ramps up at the end of the day when they finally find themselves alone with their moods. Perhaps it was Pascal, the French mathematician and philosopher, who understood this dilemma better than anyone when he observed: "All of man's miseries stem from his inability to sit alone in a room."

Although James was a genuine optimist, he was also honest enough to admit that, "It is easier to define this ideal than to give practical instructions for bringing it about."[1] What he noticed was how difficult it is to simply control what we pay attention to. Our feelings and thoughts literally seem to have "a mind of their own".

We've all had the experience of reading a book, for example, and getting to the bottom of the page before realizing we have no idea what we just read. We were actually thinking about something else entirely, while continuing to read the words on the page. Our minds are easily distracted by memories and daydreams, not to mention the persistent "to-do" list.

As frustrating as this can be at times, the more serious challenges come from the emotional turmoil in our lives caused by the unwel-come thoughts and emotions that create so much of our suffering. At any given moment, our peace of mind can be easily disturbed as we find ourselves reliving a hurtful memory or getting caught up in worry and anxiety about the future. And even when we are able to focus on the present moment clearly, we can find ourselves reacting strongly to minor irritations or disagreements with those we care about. We are easily demoralized by our circumstances or increasingly fatigued by relentless overwork.

If any of this feels like your reality, you're not alone. In a revealing study published in the November 12, 2010 issue of *Science* magazine, psychologists at Harvard University used smartphones to collect data from more than 2,000 people who were asked to report what they were doing, thinking and feeling throughout the day.

The data revealed that on any given day, while performing a range of activities, our minds are wandering about 47% of the time. And, perhaps of more concern, the study revealed that we are unhappiest when our minds are wandering, compared to when they are focused on what we're actually doing. The study's title says it all: 'A Wandering Mind Is an Unhappy Mind.' The researchers concluded: "A human mind is a wandering mind, and a wandering mind is an unhappy mind. The ability to think about what is not happening is a cognitive achievement that comes at an emotional cost."

For many of us, the personal emotional cost is tied to negative mood, psychological stress, rigid obsessional thoughts, worry, unhappiness and exhaustion.

It appears that William James was certainly ahead of his time, but he could never have imagined how his simple observation would lead ultimately to the discovery of mindfulness – one of the great scientific breakthroughs of the 21st century for dealing with these problems effectively. Nor could he have possibly known that the practical instructions for developing mindfulness were already more than 2,500 years old.

THE MINDFUL REVOLUTION

In recent years, there has been an explosion of interest in mindfulness, with widespread media coverage. In 2014, *Time* magazine introduced the year by declaring that the "Mindfulness Revolution" was here and subsequently devoted not one, but two covers to it. It sometimes seems impossible to open a magazine or a newspaper without being lectured about the stress-reducing benefits of mindfulness.

In addition to mindfulness entering the mainstream, there has been a huge increase in academic research on the subject, with more than 500 peer-reviewed scientific journal papers now being published every year.

So what exactly is mindfulness? Mindfulness is the skill of paying close attention to what's happening in the present moment in the mind, body and external environment, non-judgmentally and with an attitude of curiosity and openness. I say "skill" because the ability to do this can be developed and improved over time. In other words, you can get better at it!

I have a theory that the idea of mindfulness appeals to us because it's something that we intuitively recognize in our own experience. Whether we know it or not, we already practise it in one form or another: when we're absorbed in a hobby or sport, caring for a distressed child, or focused like a laser on solving an immediate problem at work. Rather than operating on automatic pilot, we are fully attentive to what is happening in the present moment.

The Mindfulness Book returns to the original core ideas of this 2,500-year-old practice and offers you a practical interpretation in the light of contemporary psychology's best insights about how it works.

If achieving a more peaceful and focused mind is important to you, then this book offers you a simple, time-tested path.

OVERVIEW

There's so much more to mindfulness than simply being focused on the demands of the situation right in front of us. The aim of *The Mindfulness Book* is to provide you with an easily accessible and concise guidebook for exploring and applying mindfulness to your life.

PART ONE: MINDFULNESS – EASTERN AND WESTERN SCIENCE

Part one lays the foundation by describing the essential building blocks of mindfulness: what it is, how it works and, most importantly, what it delivers. Sometimes people get confused between the terms "mindfulness" and "meditation". Essentially, meditation can be thought of as the mental training ground for developing greater mindfulness. And although a relatively simple practice, part one covers the necessary steps for putting meditation into practice so you can experience the immediate benefits. Although it's important to understand the theory behind mindfulness and meditation, nothing beats practice. I will guide you through a series of short practices so you can experience for yourself how mindfulness works.

Although the original insight that mindfulness would improve judgment, character and the quality of decision-making was made by William James, a leading philosopher and psychologist in the 19th century, the scientific data supporting the benefits of mindfulness continues to grow. In this section we will look at a representative sample of compelling scientific studies, which confirm that mindfulness and meditation are also effective in reducing a long list of stress-related diseases, enhancing the capacity of the mind to focus and sustain attention, and in cultivating a more peaceful mind and general sense of wellbeing.

PART TWO – THE PSYCHOLOGY OF MINDFULNESS

In Part One you will have begun to practise the basic skills of mindfulness that help you create psychological space for establishing a more peaceful mind. In many ways, the goals of mindfulness overlap with the objectives of cognitive psychology, and in this section we explore the core ideas of mindfulness and their relationship to cognitive psychology. In particular, we examine practical psychological strategies for using mindfulness to develop greater self-awareness and conscious control over both your state of mind and behavior.

If you've applied the lessons described in part one, you've begun to practise mindfulness, noticing your breathing, and noticing the thoughts and feelings that make up your "Self". This now raises a very interesting question: What is this part of you that does all the noticing?

In the classic tradition, when we are training the mental ability known as mindfulness, it is just as important to develop a second skill referred to as introspection. Introspection is your ability to observe your mindfulness practice – "Am I practising correctly or not?" It's a kind of quality control monitor for the entire process. Developing this skill enables you to accelerate and advance your mindfulness practice.

One of the central benefits of mindfulness is that it takes you off autopilot and opens you up to greater awareness of your experiences. By developing the ability to live more consciously in the present moment, you experience the "power of now", which means greater peace of mind, clarity, and a mind less reactive and more awake to what's going on.

By learning how to reduce the struggle with both the pleasant and unpleasant aspects of our lives, we are able to approach the whole of life with a greater lightness of being. So in part two we also ask a big question: "Is the life you are living the life you *want* to be living right now?"

Although mindfulness emphasizes approaching your personal experience non-judgmentally, this does not mean unintelligently. In fact, mindfulness and introspection are expressions of your intelligence because they guide you in becoming wiser and more discerning about where and how you direct your attention and how you behave, according to your values.

PART THREE – FOUR APPLICATIONS OF MINDFULNESS

Part of the broad appeal of mindfulness to many people is its proven effectiveness in reducing stress. This, however, is an altogether far too limited view of the potential value of mindfulness. In Part Three, we explore four powerful applications of mindfulness based on the original tradition.

Mindfulness practice almost always begins by directing our attention to the body and our immediate experience of the physical environment. Once we understand the close working relationship between the body and mind, we learn to interrupt the cause-and-effect relationship between our thoughts, feelings and our actions. Instead, we discover an increased ability to focus our mind constructively and greater power to *respond* rather than *react* to our circumstances. It is this core ability that actually forms the basis of emotional intelligence.

PART FOUR – LIVING MINDFULLY

Now that we have a better understanding of what mindfulness is and how to cultivate it, we are ready to apply its principles to affect the way we manage a range of situations in our lives. Part Four considers the challenges of living mindfully. As I mentioned earlier, part of the broad appeal of mindfulness is its effectiveness as an approach to stress management. In this section, we consider the mechanism driving the stress reaction and how a specific mindfulness technique can be used to soothe the body and calm the mind quickly. Of course, many people experience stress at work, so in this section we also consider how to apply mindfulness to a range of challenging demands in the workplace to improve performance and productivity.

The great thing about mindfulness as a skill is that it's the ultimate mobile technology. You can apply mindfulness anywhere at anytime, but it helps to have a strategy for getting the most out of your practice. So in this section we also review tips and strategies for systematically applying mindfulness and building a sustainable mindfulness practice.

Finally, why do some people achieve their potential, while most feel trapped or forced to live a life constrained by self-imposed limitations? In this final section, we apply mindfulness to the creative process to generate the conditions for a high-performing mind and for creating the life you want.

Whatever your goal, creating a more peaceful and focused mind, enjoying greater wellbeing, establishing more meaningful relationships, fulfilling your career ambitions or creating a more balanced lifestyle, *The Mindfulness Book* provides you with time-proven insights and practical strategies for living a more peaceful, productive and creative life.

BUILDING A MINDFULNESS PRACTICE

To help you develop your mindfulness practice, chapters conclude with practical takeaways in a section called '*The Practice.*' These sections provide you with mindfulness scripts or additional tips to enhance your mindfulness training. If you prefer to follow guided mindfulness sessions, you can download a range of audio files associated with each chapter from the website, www.themindfulnessbook.co.uk

PART ONE

MINDFULNESS – EASTERN AND WESTERN SCIENCE

CHAPTER 1
WHAT IS MINDFULNESS?

The aim of life is to live, and to live means to be awake, joyously, drunkenly, serenely, divinely aware.
Henry Miller, American writer, 1891-1980

Mindfulness is an ancient idea found in a wide range of spiritual traditions. It was taught more than 2,500 years ago as a mind-training technique for developing a more peaceful and focused mind, as well as for achieving greater insight into one's personal experience.

The word itself is a translation from the ancient Indian word *Sati*, which conveys two central ideas: first, that of calling to mind or remembering and second, cultivating the mind.

REMEMBERING THE PRESENT

The idea of "remembering" is not confined to past events. Rather, it's remembering to pay full attention and monitor what is happening in the mind, body and environment as it is occurring in the present moment. This is not as easy as it sounds. As we discussed in the introduction, research indicates that most of us spend a great deal of time on autopilot rather than being fully aware of our immediate experience.

While on autopilot, our thoughts are endlessly distracted, caught up with emotionally laden memories, past disappointments or future fears. So when we practise mindfulness, we remember to move off this default autopilot setting, learning instead to direct our attention and become more consciously aware of our present experience.

By remembering to pay closer attention to what is happening in the mind and body, as it is happening, the flow of cause and effect between our thoughts and our actions is potentially interrupted. This has the effect of focusing and settling the mind and creating greater peace of mind.

CULTIVATING EMOTIONAL BALANCE

The second idea behind the original meaning of mindfulness conveys the concept of "cultivating the mind". Over time, the practice of remembering to direct our attention to the present moment cultivates greater awareness and emotional balance by making the mind less vulnerable to distraction and emotional turmoil.

You can think of mindfulness as a way of resting the mind from the endless flow of thoughts and distractions that disturb your peace of mind and deplete your emotional energy. It's also a way of developing your self-awareness and self-control, that is, of increasing your emotional intelligence. This is a subject we discuss in greater detail in Chapter 14.

THREE CONTEMPORARY INSIGHTS[2]

In Western psychology, the most widely accepted definition of mindfulness is, "Paying attention to the present moment deliberately and non-judgmentally."[3] This simple definition reveals three important insights about mindfulness.

First, mindfulness is more of an *awareness* process than a *thinking* process. It involves remembering to pay attention and observe your experience rather than getting caught up in thinking about it.

Of course, there's nothing wrong with thinking. Thinking is an important part of being intelligent. But, in the same way that a fish in water may be unaware that it lives in water, we are often unaware of how much our minds are caught up in our thoughts.

If you're like most people, your mind is constantly running – like a tap that won't turn off. Each day (and night!) you experience an endless flow of thoughts and emotions, many of which have an anxious and compulsive quality to them that disturbs your peace of mind. Like a broken record that goes around and around, your mind is constantly turning over past events, wrestling with current decisions or worrying about potential future events. By being mindful, we emerge from the turbulent waters of our thought processes and create a kind of psychological observation deck. As we observe our thoughts and experience from this vantage point, we notice the water begins to settle and becomes calmer. For many, this is the first experience of the potential of mindfulness to calm the mind and soothe the body.

The second insight involves psychological flexibility – the ability to "deliberately" direct your attention to the full range of your experience. I remember vividly, as a young psychology student, being in a supervision session with my professor when his boss, the head of department, burst into the room and directed a tirade of abuse at him. His boss continued for several minutes, apparently oblivious to the inappropriateness of his behavior, particularly given my presence in the room. He left after issuing a final threat and slammed the door. A deafening silence fell for what seemed like an eternity and, of course, I felt embarrassed and self-conscious and so stood up to excuse myself. At that moment, my professor turned to me and said in a calm and totally sincere voice: "Well, he's got problems, hasn't he Mart? Now, where did we get to with this case we were discussing?" I shall never forget his complete lack of emotional reactivity to what, for most people, would be a very upsetting encounter. More than his remarkable composure, however, was his ability to restore his attention to what was of importance to him in the moment, without distraction. I recognized immediately the value of cultivating such an ability, but only years later did I understand that these skills were described in Eastern psychology as equanimity, and were integral to the cultivation of mindfulness.

In this way, mindfulness enables you to live more consciously aware of the links between how you think, feel and behave. When you are mindful, you are able to be less reactive to your experience and, instead, increase your range of responses to the challenges and opportunities you face. You are also able to become more aware of the experiences of other people and cultivate empathic connections. As your mindfulness skills improve over time, you will discover greater control over where you place your attention. This is a valuable skill for enhancing psychological resilience and increasing wellbeing.

The third insight involves the ability to suspend judgment of your circumstances and yourself. This is perhaps the most challenging aspect of applying mindfulness to daily life.

Thoughts are like the lenses through which we look at the world. We all have a tendency to hold tightly to our particular lens and allow it to determine how we interpret our experience, and even how we see ourselves. Mindfulness practice is about "letting go" of our default tendency to pass judgment and, instead, to become more comfortable with accepting "who we are" and "what life actually is".

This does not imply a passive resignation or submission to your circumstances. Instead, it suggests a willingness to allow your thoughts and feelings to be as they are, in this moment, without trying to "fix" anything. It's more about accepting your personal thoughts and feelings rather than necessarily accepting your circumstances.

Mindfulness frees you from the compulsive need to judge everything in terms of "good", "bad", "I agree", "I disagree", "I like" or "I don't like". Instead, mindfulness involves taking a more detached perspective, similar to a curious scientist. This involves adopting a more curious and less critical approach to your experience, including your relationship to yourself and other people.

Even if your experience in this moment is difficult, painful or unpleasant, mindfulness encourages you to be open to it and curious about it rather than running from it or avoiding it. This opening up to experience also involves developing greater appreciation for the whole of your experience.

In her book, *The Color Purple*, there's a wonderful moment where Alice Walker describes a scene involving Shug Avery, an African-American woman facing a particularly difficult set of circumstances. While walking through a field in the summer time, Shug remarks, "I think it pisses God off if you walk by the color purple in a field somewhere and don't notice it."

Of course, this capacity to recognize novelty and beauty in each moment characterizes the natural minds of children. Children come into the world with a natural sense of curiosity and wonder. They have no name for this "thing" and no past or current associations with it. There are no complications to cloud their perception, and they see the object in the freshest way possible.

Now, I'm not suggesting that we return to the state of innocence represented by the mind of a child, but mindfulness reminds us to look again with new eyes and discover the detail, as well as the potential for wonder and new understanding in each moment.

One of the highlights of my mindfulness workshops that I deliver to corporate clients is "The Chocolate Meditation". In this practice, participants are asked to choose a piece of chocolate or, if they prefer, a grape and mindfully enjoy it as if for the first time. As a mindfulness practice, it encourages you to remember to pay closer attention to "ordinary" experience in the present moment. As you do, the experience is potentially transformed into something quite extraordinary. Try it for yourself by either following the exercise described in "The Practice" section below or download *The Chocolate Meditation* MP3 from the website, www.themindfulnessbook.co.uk, and follow the guided version.

THE PRACTICE

The Chocolate Meditation
Choose a piece of chocolate and open the wrapper.

Now take hold of the chocolate, and observe it closely ... notice the shape, the colours, the contours ... notice the weight and how light it is in your hand ... feel the silky smooth texture against your fingers ... now smell it ... and really inhale the aroma ... and now raise it to your mouth and press it lightly against your lips ... pause for a moment before popping it in your mouth.

Close your eyes to enhance the experience ... and just notice any urges arising, perhaps the urge to bite ... but instead, hold it on your tongue and let it melt ... notice any tendency to suck it.

Explore the chocolate with your tongue, noticing the taste and the texture.

If at any time you become aware of your mind wandering while the chocolate is melting, simply notice where it went and gently bring it back to the present moment, focusing on the sweet sensations on your tongue as the chocolate melts.

Now very slowly bite into the remaining chocolate and notice the explosion of flavours and the smooth creamy texture of the chocolate as it fills your mouth.

Once the chocolate has completely melted, swallow it slowly and deliberately, and notice the remaining sweetness in your mouth.

Then, in your own time, repeat this exercise with another piece in the same way.

CHAPTER 2
MINDFULNESS
OR MEDITATION?

Look within. Within is the fountain of good, and it will ever bubble up, if you will ever dig.

Marcus Aurelius, Roman Emperor, 161-180

Okay, so remembering to pay conscious attention to the present moment, rather than living our lives on autopilot, is the first big idea behind mindfulness. It involves skills such as self-awareness, self-control and sustained concentration. I say "skills" because the ability to practice mindfulness can be developed and improved over time. This is where meditation comes in.

People often get confused between the terms "mindfulness" and "meditation" and sometimes use them interchangeably or combine them, such as "mindfulness meditation". Generally, when people speak or write about mindfulness in the media, they avoid reference to the term "meditation". Typically this is either out of ignorance or concern that people have long associated the term with religious ideas such as those found in Buddhism and other Eastern religions. The term mindfulness carries none of this brand baggage and so makes it more acceptable and, therefore, more accessible to the people in the West.

Nevertheless, as we know, both mindfulness and meditation have ancient origins that predate Buddhism and have been practiced for thousands of years. As mind-training techniques, they don't depend on any particular religious or philosophical ideas, but I'm convinced that appreciating the origins of these practices, and how they relate to each other, helps clarify how they work.

MEDITATION OR MINDFULNESS?

The word "meditation" itself is a translation from the ancient Indian word *bhavana*, which simply means "cultivation". If mindfulness is remembering to pay attention to the present moment, then meditation is the training ground for cultivating mindfulness.

There are a great many varieties of meditation practices, but according to the Tibetan tradition, they fall into one of two groups. The first is "stabilizing" meditation (Sanskrit: *shamata*), in which the aim is to develop a stable, concentrated mind. This type of meditation is great for developing concentration, calming a busy mind and lowering stress. It involves fixing your mind on an object of meditation, such as the breath, and developing the skill to hold it there single-pointedly for a period of time. In this sense, meditation is actually a form of mindfulness. In fact, according to one of the world's most authoritative mindfulness scholars, Alan Wallace, "Mindfulness is a foundation for all other kinds of meditation."[4]

The second type of meditation is "analytical" (Sanskrit: *vipashyana*) meditation. This is useful for developing insight or for familiarizing yourself with how your mind thinks and how you behave. By calming your mind and observing your thoughts, feelings and behavior more dispassionately, you examine the causes and consequences of your experience more clearly and cultivate greater psychological mindedness.

Of course, the two broad approaches to meditation – stabilizing and analytical meditation – complement one another and can be used together. And although mindfulness is traditionally associated with practising analytical meditation, of course it helps if we have well-developed attention skills. These are developed through practising stabilizing meditation. So, the practice of fixing your attention on an object, such as the breath or a visual or mental image, and holding it there consistently over a period of time, lays the foundation for greater mindfulness. Perhaps this is more clearly understood through an analogy.

THE WANDERING ELEPHANT AND THE ROPE

In ancient India, the mind was sometimes compared to a wild, unrestrained elephant that wandered the countryside. A wandering, wild elephant posed a potential threat to local villages and so attempts were made to capture and train it. The analogy is clear. A wandering, untamed mind can inflict enormous damage and is the primary threat to our peace of mind and happiness.

Meditation was understood to be like training an elephant. In the same way that an elephant is trained by tethering it to a stake in the ground, so the mind is trained by tethering it to a fixed object such as the breath or a particular sound or an image. But how do you tether your mind to the object? By the rope of mindfulness that, as we know, involves continuously remembering the object.

In other words, when we practise meditation, we focus single-pointedly on an object, and whenever we notice that our attention has strayed, we return it over and over again to the object for an extended period of time. Sooner or later, the mind stops pacing and calms down. Eventually, with practice, the elephant finally sits down and the mind experiences a greater sense of tranquillity, clarity and wellbeing.

JUST ONE MORE THING

The final point in the analogy is that the elephant tamer has an iron hook with which he or she prods the elephant whenever it tries to stray away. This is analogous to a tool described in the mindfulness traditions as "introspection" (Sanskrit: *sampajanna*), which we discuss in more detail in Chapter 7.

As you practise mindfulness of the breath, for example, introspection is the knack of noticing when your mind has been distracted by thoughts and has lost focus on the breath. Western psychology also recognises this ability and refers to it as metacognition, which means "above" or "beyond thinking". You can think of it operating a bit like a quality-control mechanism that provides continuous feedback to you on how your mindfulness practice is going. "*Am I still focused on the breath? Am I remembering to relax my body? Am I aware of the sense of stillness around me?*"

SUMMARY

The overall approach of this type of meditation is to relax the body and develop a peaceful, stable mind that can concentrate for longer and longer periods without losing focus. This type of meditation not only builds concentration, it also reduces mental chatter, emotional turmoil and lowers stress.

The regular practice of meditation, even for a few minutes a day, supports the development of greater mindfulness. As we train ourselves to pay attention to the breath, we are developing a skill that can be generalized to our lives. For example, we also improve our ability to pay attention to the person speaking to us, or to enjoying our meal or drinking a cup of coffee, or as you experienced in the previous chapter, eating chocolate!

As a clinical psychologist, I'm only too well aware of the critical importance of attention to wellbeing and emotional balance. A mind prone to distraction is vulnerable to a range of negative and stressful emotional states. Among other benefits, meditation offers a method for achieving extraordinary concentration and is an important practice for enhancing mindfulness.

That's the theory – now try a short meditation practice for yourself. You can begin by following the exercise described in "The Practice" section below or download the One-Minute Meditation MP3 from the website, www.themindfulnessbook.co.uk, and follow the guided version.

THE PRACTICE

One-Minute Meditation
Let's begin with a short, one-minute meditation practice.

Find a comfortable position. Whether you're sitting on a chair or cross-legged on a cushion, sit with your back straight in a comfortable posture.

Allow your shoulders to relax and let your hands rest comfortably in your lap. Let your eyes close or simply lower your gaze, unfocused.

Just for a minute, allow your body to relax and your mind to rest.

Allow your awareness to descend into the entire field of the body. Simply become aware of the physical sensations as you experience them in your body. Let all the muscles of your body become loose and limp.

Bring your awareness to the sensations of breathing. Without trying to control the breath in any way, just allow your body to breathe. Let your breath find its own natural rhythm.

Allow each out-breath to feel like a sigh of relief ... and continue to release any excess tension and tightness. With each breath, allow yourself to become more and more relaxed, more and more comfortable.

If after a while you notice that your mind has wandered, this is normal. Simply relax, let go of the thought or image, and gently return your attention to the sensation of the breath.

Now allow your eyes to open and become aware of your surroundings. Notice how you feel.

CHAPTER 3
HOW TO MEDITATE

All men's miseries derive from not being able to sit in a quiet room alone.
Blaise Pascal, French mathematician and philosopher

As I suggested in the previous chapter, meditation is the training ground for cultivating greater mindfulness. So this chapter describes how to practise what is possibly the most widely practiced meditation in the world – mindfulness of breathing.

If you're like most people, you're busy and caught up with so many things happening around you in your family or at work. It can be quite a challenge to stop for a few minutes and turn your attention inward. But there's something else going on besides simply being busy. As Blaise Pascal, described it: "All men's miseries derive from not being able to sit in a quiet room alone." I possibly wouldn't go as far as Pascal, but it's true that many people find it excruciating to sit for long in a quiet room without becoming agitated or bored. We're so addicted to external stimulation that we're often not comfortable turning inward, so we keep ourselves stimulated and distracted by a variety of means.

THE MOTIVE

The first decision you'll need to make to begin practising meditation and cultivating mindfulness is to be clear about your motivation.

What would you like to achieve by your practice? Without setting lofty or even noble goals initially, it's simply important to be honest with yourself. Perhaps your motive is as general as to improve your life through increased concentration, or to calm yourself to deal with a difficult relationship, or maybe you want to reduce your susceptibility to stress and increase your resilience at work.

At some point in your development, you'll discover that your practice of mindfulness moves you beyond a focus on yourself to a broader focus on how your practice can be of value to others. We explore this in more detail in Chapter 10, but for now, living mindfully involves the decision to be on good terms with both yourself and with others wherever possible. So as you come to this practice, take a kindly approach to yourself. Like any skill worth developing, it takes consistent effort and persistence to enjoy the benefits. This is particularly true of mindfulness and meditation because it is counter-intuitive to all of your previous conditioning.

MEDITATION IN THREE EASY STEPS

So that you can get straight into the practice, I've provided you with an overview of a simple three-step process below, as well as a script to follow in "The Practice" section at the end of the chapter. Alternatively, once you've reviewed it, you may like to go the website, www.themindfulnessbook.co.uk, and download the *Mindfulness of Breathing – Short Practice* MP3 and follow the guided version.

GETTING STARTED

Find a quiet, private place where you won't be disturbed for a few minutes, and decide how much time you will spend meditating.

I'd recommend allowing at least three to six minutes to complete the three-step practice described here.

The instructions for basic meditation are really incredibly simple and to help you remember this basic practice, I've broken it down into just three steps.

STEP 1. RELAX THE BODY

Begin by relaxing your body. It's preferable to practise meditation sitting on a chair or cushion, but you can lie on your back if you prefer. Whatever position you choose, make sure that your back is straight and your shoulders are relaxed. Your head should be resting comfortably, with your head tilted slightly forward. This takes the pressure off your neck if you're sitting upright. You can close your eyes or leave them partially open, as you wish, but remember to relax and soften the muscles of your face. Allow your hands to rest comfortably in your lap or beside you if you're lying down.

Although many people find mindfulness training a very pleasant and relaxing experience, it's important to realize that, in and of itself, relaxation is actually not the goal or the end game of meditation practice. Establishing a relaxed body is simply a doorway to developing a quiet and calm mind. Once the body is relaxed, the mind can calm down. Relaxing the body, then, becomes a powerful tool for the cultivation of mindfulness.

Now simply bring your awareness to the physical sensations throughout your body. Notice the sensations in your shoulders and neck, or back, and continue to scan your entire body. Wherever you find tightness or tension, simply relax and allow your body to settle into a posture of ease and comfort.

STEP 2. STABILIZE THE BREATHING

Some people find it helpful at this point to take three long, slow, deep breaths, remembering not only to relax deeply with each out breath, but also to let go of any distracting thoughts or feelings.

Next, become aware of your breathing. And at least initially, without trying to influence your breath in any way at all, simply observe the in and out flow of the breath for a few seconds, wherever you experience it in the body. Pay particular attention to the physical sensations that you experience as your abdomen expands and contracts.

After a minute or so, notice how your breathing has become slower and perhaps longer and deeper. I'll explain more about the process of why this occurs in the next chapter. But for now, the most important focus here is simply to observe the breath as it flows automatically.

Notice the entire course of each in and out breath, keeping as physically still as you can while allowing your respiration to flow effortlessly, as if you were fast asleep.

STEP 3. FOCUS THE MIND

Now pay particular attention to the breath as you experience it around your abdomen. Notice the sensation of breath as the abdomen expands and contracts. Perhaps you notice a slight stretching sensation as the air expands your abdomen. Pay close attention to these sensations.

If, after a while, you notice that your mind has wandered and started to think, this is normal. In general, almost everyone experiences mental chatter the first time they practise silent meditation – it's noisy in there. This is called excitement or, more traditionally, gross agitation and it happens to everybody. When it does, and as soon as you realize your mind has wandered, let your first thought be simply to relax. Let go of the thought or image and gently return your attention to the sensation of the breath around your abdomen.

On the other hand, for some people, particularly some corporate people I work with, they are often so tired that instead of being distracted by excitement or gross agitation, they lose concentration and experience drowsiness or "dullness" on the way to falling asleep. Once again, this is normal, particularly if you're tired. As soon as you become aware of having lost clarity or sharpness of focus, lift your chest, inhale sharply and return your focus to the breath. This action stimulates the sympathetic nervous system, which heightens alertness.

Finish the session by taking three long, slow, deep breaths. Breathing through the nose, all the way down deeply into the abdomen, filling the belly and allowing the chest to expand. Then breathe out again, effortlessly releasing the breath while being mindfully attentive to the sensations throughout the body.

Now allow your eyes to open and become fully aware of your surroundings, and notice how you feel.

SUMMING UP

Everyone's experience of this initial practice is quite different. Some people find it very relaxing and recognize immediately the calming effects. Others find it very difficult to calm the mind and find themselves easily distracted or agitated, and some become instantly sleepy. Whatever your experience, the key here is practice. Decide not to "beat up" on yourself because you've tried a few times and still experience gross agitation. With regular short practice sessions, in which you focus on the element of relaxation, if nothing else you will experience increasing calm and your mind will learn to settle. If you're getting drowsy quickly, try changing the time of day when you practise. Many people find their minds fresher and less distracted just after waking up in the mornings.

In the next chapter I'll provide additional techniques that help stabilize your focus and deepen your experience.

That's the theory – now try a short meditation practice for yourself. You can begin by following the exercise described in "The Practice" section below or download the One-Minute Meditation MP3 from the website, www.themindfulnessbook.co.uk, and follow the guided version.

THE PRACTICE

Mindfulness of Breathing Meditation – Short Practice
Let's begin with a short practice of mindfulness of breathing.

Find a comfortable position. Whether you're sitting on a chair or cross-legged on a cushion, sit with your back straight in a comfortable posture.

Allow your shoulders to relax and let your hands rest comfortably in your lap. Allow your eyes to close or simply lower your gaze, unfocused, a few feet in front of you.

Know that as you come to this session, you can set aside all other concerns and responsibilities and the things that occupy your mind. Just like putting down a heavy bag, just for a few minutes ... allow your body to relax and your mind to rest ... just for a few minutes.

Allow your awareness to descend into the entire field of the body. Simply become aware of the physical sensations as you experience them in your body. Let all the muscles of your body become loose and limp.

Bring your awareness to the sensations of breathing. And without trying to control the breath in any way, allow your body to breathe. Whether it's fast or slow, long or short, just let it flow effortlessly, rhythmically and automatically.

Let your breath find its own natural rhythm.

Allow each out breath to feel like a sigh of relief ... and continue to release any excess tension and tightness. With each breath, allow yourself to become more and more relaxed, more and more comfortable.

CHAPTER 4
MINDFULNESS
OF BREATHING

When you own your breath, nobody can steal your peace.

Author Unknown

In the previous chapter, I introduced a three-step overview of a simple meditation process for mindfulness training. Many approaches to training mindfulness focus on the breath. Consciously bringing your awareness to your breath is an easy way to take it off your thoughts and a very safe place to put it.

BREATHE AS IF YOUR LIFE DEPENDS ON IT

As a resting place, refuge and anchor for your attention, the breath is always accessible – it is, quite literally, right under your nose. And although simple and relatively straightforward, mindfulness of breathing is an extremely powerful technique for training the mind and cultivating the positive benefits of mindfulness. There are several reasons for this.

First, breathing is continuous and something you do automatically, without conscious control, until something either restricts your breathing or someone draws your attention to it. For example, you probably were completely unaware of your breathing until you began reading these words in the last few minutes. So breathing is not something that we need to control unless we choose to and, as such, it can be a conscious or unconscious act and provides a convenient object for training awareness.

Second, breathing also functions as a powerful connection between the mind and body. At the unconscious level, breathing is a bodily function that occurs automatically, thanks to the autonomic nervous system.

The autonomic or involuntary nervous system has two divisions: On the one hand, the sympathetic branch prepares the body for emergencies; it increases heart rate and blood pressure, for example. On the other hand, the parasympathetic nervous system has precisely the opposite effect: it slows the heart rate and also lowers blood pressure.

Interestingly, when we inhale, we directly stimulate the sympathetic nervous system, whereas when we exhale we directly stimulate the parasympathetic nervous system. These two systems are intended to work in balance, and once they get out of balance we experience the physical and emotional symptoms associated with stress. We discuss this in more detail in Chapter 15, in which I also describe a powerful mindful breathing technique that is the most effective refuge from stress and anxiety that I know. In the long term, this technique works to help soothe the body and calm the mind by bringing these two systems back into balance.

Third, your breath is also influenced by your emotional state and shaped by your moods. Your emotions change the way you breathe. When you're anxious, afraid or angry, your breathing is always fast and shallow. Whereas, when you're relaxed and in a calm state of mind, your breathing is slower and deeper. The good news is that by changing the way that you breathe, you can also change your emotions.

As a clinical psychologist, it's rarely effective to tell patients who are distressed to "calm down". It is much more effective to help them focus on making their breathing slower, deeper and more regular. This almost always has the immediate effect of calming their emotional state. The effectiveness of this approach is greatly enhanced by shifting the focus of the breath from the chest to the abdomen.

FILLING THE POT FROM THE BOTTOM UP

When we were very young, we tended to breathe using our diaphragm. This had the effect of expanding the abdomen rather than the chest. For various reasons, over time most of us have allowed our breathing to become shallower and tend to breathe using the muscles around the chest. As a result, we restrict our capacity to take a full, deep breath.

Simply by shifting your breathing to the diaphragm and allowing the abdomen to expand first, followed by the chest, you cultivate a more mindful approach to breathing. In Eastern traditions, this is described as "filling the pot from the bottom up." It takes some practice, and you may like to place your hand on the abdomen to check if you're getting it right. This has the effect of slowing and deepening the breath and allowing you to take the full volume of air into your lungs.

As you cultivate greater awareness of your breath, it can function as an emotional barometer, helping you monitor and regulate your emotional states. In this way, your breath can also function as a kind of emotional anchor for managing your state of mind.

FROM MANAGING TO MONITORING

As effective as learning to manage your breathing can be in regulating your physiology and emotional state, mindfulness of breathing involves doing nothing other than simply paying attention to your breath; that is, not trying to change the rhythm, not trying to speed it up or slow it down, simply observing it. This is the first step and the very simplest form of settling your mind.

This is something that you can do any time – you can do it waiting in line at the airport or at the checkout, or while driving your car, or you can do it while sitting and listening to a presentation. You can think of mindfulness of breathing as a way of resting the mind and taking a short mental break from the endless flow of thoughts and emotions that capture your attention.

Building on your experience with the three-step meditation process practiced in the previous chapter, we now add a fourth step to help you stabilise your attention on the breath, by adding a dimension of vividness. This also has the effect of sharpening the focus of attention and settling the mind. Many people find this additional step a key factor in moving from an agitated mind to a more settled experience.

So that you can get straight into the practice, I've provided a short overview of the four-step process in the "The Practice" section below. Once you've reviewed it, you may like to download the *Mindfulness of Breathing Meditation – Extended Practice* MP3 from the website and follow the guided version.

In the following chapters, I'll provide you with additional techniques that help you stabilize your focus and deepen your experience. But in the next chapter, we'll explore what science says about the benefits you can expect from practising mindfulness.

That's the theory – now try a short meditation practice for yourself. You can begin by following the exercise described in "The Practice" section below or download the One-Minute Meditation MP3 from the website, www.themindfulnessbook.co.uk, and follow the guided version.

THE PRACTICE

Mindfulness of Breathing Meditation – Extended Practice (8 -10 minutes)

Getting Started
It is generally preferable to practice mindfulness of breathing sitting comfortably in a chair or on a cushion. Sit comfortably with your back straight, and relax your body. Wear comfortable clothing, or if you're in business attire, loosen your clothing so that it doesn't restrict your waist and so as not to be distracted by any temporary discomfort. Ensure that you will not be disturbed for at least fifteen minutes.

Step 1. Relax Your Body
If you are sitting, rest your hands on your knees or in your lap. Your eyes can be closed or you can keep them open, as you

wish. Now scan your body from the soles of your feet to the top of your head and make sure each part is relaxed, including your face. Note the sensations in your body and if you detect any tightness, release it.

Step 2. Take Three Breaths

Once you have settled your body, take three long, slow, gentle breaths, breathing in and out through the nostrils. Allow your breath to fill the lower part of your lungs first, pushing your abdomen out. With each out breath, allow yourself to relax more deeply.

Step 3. Watch Your Breath

Now settle your breathing in its natural flow, letting it flow automatically without attempting to control it or change it – just as if you were asleep. Simply observe the inflow and outflow of breath around the abdomen and stay focused on that sensation. When thoughts arise to distract you, as they inevitably will, instead of tensing up, simply let them go and return your attention to your breath.

Step 4. Elevate Your Attention

Now elevate your attention to the base of the nostrils, or upper lip. Notice the sensation of breath at the base of the nostrils. Perhaps you are able to notice the slightly cool sensation of the air on the inhalation and the warm air on the exhalation. Pay close attention to these sensations. Simply follow the sensations all the way to the end of the exhalation, then all the way in to the top of the inhalation.

Once you attempt this, you will be surprised how difficult it is to remain focused on your breathing for even a few seconds before being distracted by thoughts of things to do. One technique you can use to help calm your distracted mind is to count your breaths.

Try counting "one" at the beginning of your first inhalation, then attending closely to the sensations of your breathing through the rest of the inhalation and the entire exhalation. Count "two" at the beginning of the next breath, and continue. Your goal is to reach ten breaths. However, each time you become aware that you have become distracted by a thought or a memory and your mind has wandered, return your count to "one".

Practise this for a few minutes at least twice a day until you can consistently reach ten breaths without distraction – be patient and persistent and watch your progress. It may take a while, but you'll get there. Notice how you feel at the end of each practice. Your breathing has slowed, your body is more relaxed, your mind is calmer, and you are ready to return to your responsibilities with a more peaceful mind.

CHAPTER 5
BENEFITS OF MINDFULNESS

The greatest discovery of my generation is that human beings can alter their lives by altering their attitude of mind. . . . If you change your mind, you can change your life.

William James

I was recently watching a rerun of the movie *Limitless*, starring Bradley Cooper, about an out-of-work writer who discovers a top-secret designer drug that bestows him with super-human abilities. The drug allows him to use 100% of his mind and makes him laser-focused and more confident than any person alive.

It's a seductive idea and the stuff of science fiction. But what if you were offered a pill that you could take once a day that could reduce anxiety and depressed mood, increase your energy levels, and enhance the capacity of your mind to focus and improve decision-making?

Well, a review of the scientific literature for the past 15 years suggests that the psychological equivalent of that pill may exist. It's called mindfulness. Although the scientific literature is a mixture of both good and bad science, the overall findings are quite remarkable.

HARD DATA – SOFT SKILLS

I recently met with one of the main contributors to the growing body of scientific literature on mindfulness, Richard Davidson, a leading neuroscientist from the University of Wisconsin-Madison. According to Davidson, *"There is nothing soft about this data."* He refers to a long list of scientific publications over the last 15 years documenting the effectiveness of mindfulness in treating both psychological conditions such as depression and anxiety, as well as physical outcomes such as chronic pain and stress-related diseases.

There's now more than 500 studies published a year on the effectiveness of mindfulness. In this chapter I will focus on some of the big meta-analyses that summarize large numbers of studies in three areas: stress management, attention and focus, and anxiety management.

THE SCIENCE

Research into the effectiveness of mindfulness from a psychological and medical perspective really gained momentum following the work of Jon Kabat-Zinn from the University of Massachusetts Medical School. Kabat-Zinn developed an outpatient programme called "Mindfulness-Based Stress Reduction" (MBSR).

The eight-week MBSR programme emphasizes two aspects of attention: first, the ability to voluntarily *focus* attention and second, the ability to *monitor* ongoing thoughts, feelings and sensations – without getting caught up in them. This mental monitoring is a process called meta-cognition, or introspection, and I discuss it further in Chapter 7. Together, both processes help prevent our minds from wandering on automatic pilot. The MBSR programme has been associated with a range of positive physical and psychological outcomes.

STRESS MANAGEMENT

While moderate levels of stress can enhance performance, excessive or prolonged levels of stress can increase the risk of a range of physical and mental health conditions, as well as decrease performance on a variety of tasks. Most people who practice mindfulness and meditation regularly report feeling less stressed and more emotionally balanced.

Our levels of physical and mental arousal are largely governed by the autonomic nervous system that, as we discussed in Chapter 4, has two divisions. On the one hand, the sympathetic branch prepares the body for emergencies through the "fight-or-flight" response, which increases heart rate and blood pressure, among other functions. Chronic mild to moderate activation of the fight-or-flight response through excessive worrying can be extremely damaging to the body. On the other hand, the parasympathetic nervous system has precisely the opposite effect: it slows the heart rate and also lowers blood pressure.

Mindfulness and meditation activate the parasympathetic system, the "rest and digest" part of our nervous system, helping with stress management. This is sometimes referred to as the "relaxation response."

According to neuroscientists like Richard Davidson, the stress response is initiated in the amygdala, the part of the brain responsible for triggering fear and anxiety. A study performed at Stanford University found that an eight-week mindfulness course reduced the reactivity of the amygdala and increased activity in areas of the prefrontal cortex that help regulate emotions, subsequently reducing stress.[5]

In one of the early studies conducted by both Davidson and Kabat-Zinn, stressed employees at a biotechnology company undertook a programme of mindfulness training. The study revealed that after just eight weeks of training, participants' stress and anxiety levels dropped significantly.[6] Furthermore, a meta-analysis of studies in nonclinical populations indicated that MBSR could significantly reduce stress in comparison to control conditions.[7] An avalanche of recent data suggests that mindfulness practice works to help sooth the body and calm the mind. I will discuss the physiological and psychological mechanisms behind stress in more detail in Chapter 15, as well as introduce the relaxing mindful breath technique. This method works powerfully to increase the activity of the parasympathetic system and is designed to provide you with an effective refuge from stress and anxiety.

ANXIETY

One of the specific features associated with stress is the experience of pervasive anxiety. Many professional people I work with frequently describe experiencing anxiety each evening along with an inability to calm themselves down. Many resort to drinking alcohol or watching TV to distract themselves.

Numerous scientific studies have found meditation to be effective for treating anxiety. Researchers in the US reviewed the literature examining how mindfulness had helped with anxiety management across a range of people, from those dealing with cancer to those suffering from social anxiety and eating disorders. They examined 39 scientific studies totalling 1,140 participants and concluded that mindfulness reduced anxiety across a wide range of conditions and that the skills associated with mindfulness could be generalized and applied to deal with stress in general.[8]

Other research includes a recent meta-analysis of 209 studies with a total of 12,145 participants. It concluded that mindfulness practice showed "Large and clinically significant effects in treating anxiety and depression, and the gains were maintained at follow-up."[9]

Perhaps it's not surprising that, if mindfulness reduces anxiety and depression, it's also been consistently found to contribute to improving wellbeing, including optimism, empathy, sense of cohesion, self-compassion and overall quality of life.[10]

ATTENTION AND FOCUS

In addition to improving health conditions, studies have shown that mindfulness improves the ability of the mind to focus and sustain attention. This leads to improvements in decision-making, executive control and performance at work. Of course, this finding is of particular interest to organizations that are struggling to tackle issues arising from increased complexity and pressure in the workplace. Not surprisingly, high-profile global corporations such as Google and Sky, among many others, have an extensive commitment to providing mindfulness training across the organization.

For the last two years, we've been running a mindfulness-based emotional intelligence programme at Sky called "Better Self". What's interesting about the "Better Self" programme is that its primary objective is not improving stress-management skills. It's more about providing leaders with skills to support the development of a high-performing mind. Participants do report feeling calmer, but also report being better able to concentrate for longer periods of time without becoming distracted. These anecdotal reports are supported by a number of randomized controlled trials of mindfulness-based interventions.[11]

A 2012 US study examined how meditation training affected individuals' behavior in multitasking at work. The researchers found that, compared with the people who didn't meditate, "Those trained in meditation stayed on tasks longer and made fewer task switches, as well as reported less negative feedback after task performance."[12] Objective measures indicate that even brief periods of mindfulness practice can lead to higher cognitive skills such as improved reaction times, comprehension scores, working memory functioning and decision-making.[13]

TAKING A BREATHER

In this chapter I've summarized, all too briefly, some of the vast amount of data supporting the benefits of practicing mindfulness in just three areas. This is only the beginning. If you're like me, you may wish to explore the data more closely. For a more comprehensive review of the research examining the benefits of mindfulness in the areas of health, education, the workplace and the criminal justice system, I recommend obtaining a copy of the UK government report "Mindful Nation UK".

So, let's take a breather and conclude this chapter by once again returning to a focus on mindfulness practice and, once again, centering our attention on the breath.

As you practised the mindfulness of breathing exercise described in the previous chapter, you may have found it quite challenging to maintain focus on your breathing for more than a few breaths. The good news is that if you practice for just a few minutes a day, you will find that you're able to hold your attention for longer and longer periods. But for those of you who would appreciate some additional help, in "The Practice" section on this page I introduce an alternative-breath counting method that you may prefer.

In the *Nine-Cycle Breathing Meditation*, we alternate the focus of the inhalation and exhalation on each nostril. And, because it's slightly busier, many people find it much easier to maintain their focus. Think of it as adding training wheels that help stabilize your mindfulness of breathing practice. Once again, the guided version can be downloaded from www.themindfulnessbook.co.uk.

THE PRACTICE

Nine-Cycle Breathing Meditation
In this session, we begin by relaxing the body and stabilizing the breath. Know that as you come to this meditation session, you can set aside all other concerns and responsibilities and the things that occupy your mind.

Settle yourself into a comfortable position, either sitting on a chair or cushion or lying on a mat ... allow your abdominal muscles to feel loose, so that when you breathe you can feel the breath go right down to the abdomen and feel your belly expand with each inhalation. Relax your shoulders, with your hands resting comfortably in your lap or by your sides.

Allow your eyes to close or, if you prefer, leave your eyes partially open, and simply lower your gaze, unfocused, to an area in front of you. Let all of the muscles of your body become loose and limp, and settle your body into a posture of ease and comfort.

Now bring your attention to the base of your nostrils and observe the sensations of breath flowing in and flowing out at the base of your nostrils. You may notice a distinctly cool sensation to the breath on the inhalation and that the breath is slightly warmed on the exhalation.

While keeping the face soft and relaxed, continue to observe these subtle sensations of the movement of the air in and out. Remember to relax deeply on each out breath, and refocus and crystalize your attention again with each in breath.

Now focus your attention on the sensation of inhaling through your left nostril and exhaling through your right nostril for three breaths. Of course, this is difficult to do without blocking the nostril but, to the best of your ability, do this beginning with the left nostril.

Now reverse this process by inhaling through your right nostril and exhaling through your left nostril for three breaths. Finally, inhale and exhale through both nostrils for three breaths.

Continue to practice this nine-cycle breathing meditation on your own for a full nine breaths. Begin with the inhalation through the left nostril. Remember to relax deeply with each out breath; perhaps notice the pause at the end of the breath and arouse your awareness of the sensation of the air at the base of the nostril on each in breath.

In this way, you complete a full cycle of meditation with each respiratory cycle. If, at some point, you notice that your attention has wandered away from the breath, either caught up in thought or images ... simply let go of the thought or image and gently return your attention back to the breath at the base of your nostril, and continue your nine-cycle count. Mindfully attend to the breath.

Now let's conclude the session. Allow your eyes to open and become fully aware of your surroundings and notice how you feel - relaxed body, calm mind.

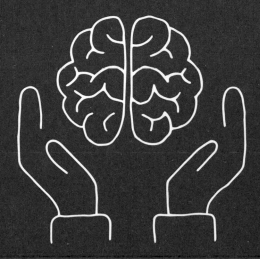

PART TWO

THE PSYCHOLOGY OF MINDFULNESS

CHAPTER 6
LOSING YOURSELF AND FINDING YOUR "SELF"

Compared to what we ought to be, we are half awake.

William James

Know thyself.

Thales, Greek philosopher

In many ways, the goals of mindfulness overlap with many of the objectives of cognitive psychology; that is, to increase freedom of choice, psychological flexibility and emotional balance. This is not surprising, given that the Eastern philosophical tradition that provides the background to mindfulness can equally be thought of as a practical psychology.

If I asked you who you are, what would you say? You might begin by telling me what you do for work – teacher, lawyer or accountant, for example. But that's the work you do, not who you are. What would happen if you changed or lost your job? That identity would disappear, but you'd still exist. So who is the "self" you are referring to?

Because I'm a psychologist, you might start telling me about your personality, or core aspects of your character or values. But these describe the ways you behave or what motivates you. They don't capture who you are, your "self". As you push this line of questioning further, it becomes clear how difficult it is to identify a permanent, fixed idea of your "self".

I THINK THEREFORE ... ?

In fact, the Eastern philosophical tradition behind mindfulness pushes it all the way and challenges the very Western idea that the "self" we refer to as our identity actually exists! They prefer to argue instead that there is, in reality, "no self". Of course, this isn't suggesting we don't exist physically. Obviously, our bodies feel pain. Yes, we exist! Rather, what it's really saying is that the "self" that we refer to when we think about ourselves or describe ourselves to others doesn't exist as a permanent, independent identity. This sense of "self" is in some way connected to everything else and is constantly changing and, therefore, hard to pin down.

Now, I don't want to get bogged down in deep, philosophical discussion here, you know, "If a tree falls in the forest ...?" In fact, Western psychology prefers the more rational approach, such as René Descartes' maxim, "I think, therefore I am." But even cognitive psychology is prepared to concede that the "self" doing the thinking, our identity, is at least socially constructed and therefore constantly evolving. This is also a powerful idea behind mindfulness.

YOU HAVEN'T CHANGED A BIT!

We all have a story about who we are and it includes some information about our occupation, gender, family background, relationship status and so on. These ideas, or "self structures" as psychologists refer to them, are the building blocks of our minds and, to a large extent, our personalities. They have been shaped by the genes we were born with and countless events to which we've developed some fairly predictable responses.

It's one of the reasons why, when you show up at school reunions and catch up with people you haven't seen for twenty years, they say things like, "You haven't changed a bit" or "I'd recognize you anywhere." Of course, in the main, they're referring to the familiar elements of your personality that they recognize.

To realize how fragile this idea of the "self" that you're attached to is, you only have to imagine what would have happened to you if you'd been switched at birth. Imagine that you'd been raised in a completely different environment, with different parents and different life events. How completely different your mind and sense of "self" would likely be today.

This isn't to say that your sense of "self" isn't useful. Despite its limitations, your current sense of "self", including your personality, has determined how you think, feel and behave over the course of your life. In this way, it has helped you achieve all that you've accomplished to date. So let's refer to it as Self with a capital "S".

But if you buy into this story completely by holding on to it too tightly, you begin thinking of this Self as having an independent existence. You know, ideas such as, "I *am* these thoughts" or "I *am* these feelings," rather than "I *have* these thoughts and feelings." This can leave you very vulnerable when life doesn't work out exactly as you might have planned, or when life challenges your idea of what a successful Self means.

At the very least, when you attach rigidly or, more accurately, defensively to these ideas about your Self, it potentially sets you up for rigid and defensive ways of responding to changes that occur in your personal and professional lives. This limits the range of responses you can generate to deal with life's opportunities and challenges. You're likely to find yourself coping with stress or negative emotions, managing relationship challenges, work pressures or conflict in exactly the same ineffective ways as you've always done.

Many of the disappointing behaviors that you notice in yourself (or, more to the point, that others notice!) are often the consequence of this rigid, defensive pattern of responses.

PLEASED TO MEET YOU ... ER, I MEAN ME!

You can think of mindfulness as a special lens that allows you to examine your self-concept closely. It encourages you to let go of the stories and "self structures" that have rigidly defined you and, instead, pay attention to the potential of the choices you're faced with right now. In other words, mindfulness invites you to change the fundamental way you relate to your inner experiences, including your relationship to your Self.

Of course, this doesn't mean that you forget about all the valuable lessons you've learned from your past. But mindfulness addresses the real question: "How are those things actually influencing me in this moment?" And, more importantly, "How can I make more positive choices by changing my view of the situation?"

The idea is to become open to authoring a new story and responding in new ways that may be more effective in dealing with your circumstances. In effect, this is the basic skill for increasing self-awareness and self-control and for building your emotional intelligence, a topic we deal with in Chapter 13.

So the philosophical idea of "no self" that lies behind mindfulness is not that dissimilar to the idea of the "social self" within cognitive psychology. Both ideas teach us to let go of our egos and to rely less on our personal stories to give us security.

Yes, you still have your sense of Self, but through mindfulness, the way you relate to your Self really changes. In light of this, I find mindfulness a profoundly optimistic practice because it suggests that we have more positive potential to change ourselves and our influence in ways we may never have considered possible.

MOVING FROM "ME" TO "WE"

According to the mindfulness tradition, it's this preoccupation with the Self that is one of the root causes of our suffering. Not only do we struggle to accept ourselves, but as we view ourselves as fundamentally independent and separate from others, we set up conditions for conflict with others. By viewing ourselves as intimately connected and interdependent with all other people, as well as with all phenomena in the world, we establish the conditions for a more compassionate world.

Mindfulness reminds you that the idea you have of your Self is the result of the complex interplay of the genes you were born with, life circumstances, and chance events and encounters, many of which have been beyond your control. It encourages you to see your suffering and the suffering of others as interconnected.

Although there is some contention about whether it was Plato, Philo of Alexandria, or John Watson who said it, perhaps the implications of this have been captured best in the statement: "Be kind, for everyone you meet is fighting a hard battle." The fact is that by recognizing the suffering of others as similar to our own suffering, we can approach both others and ourselves less judgmentally and with greater kindness. This is a major step toward greater freedom and peace of mind.

THE PRACTICE

✓ When you turn inwardly to examine yourself, whatever you find, don't judge it, but learn to observe it or even like it.

✓ When experiencing pain or failure, instead of being stridently self-critical, treat yourself with the same kindness and understanding as you would others.

✓ Mindfully observe your negative experiences without identifying with them so personally.

✓ Decide to accept yourself more completely, realizing that today you may not be all that you would like to be, but that you're not what you were yesterday.

✓ Resist comparing yourself to others. Instead, view what happens to you as part of the broader human experience rather than something that's specifically all about you.

✓ Catch yourself smiling at the voice in your head as you would at the antics of a child.

✓ As we become more mindful at watching thoughts arrive and dissolve, we recognize that all the thoughts we have ever had, including thoughts of Self, are transient. Don't sweat the small stuff!

CHAPTER 7
THE OBSERVING SELF – NOW THAT'S INTERESTING

The moment one gives close attention to anything, even a blade of grass, it becomes a mysterious, awesome, indescribably magnificent world in itself."

Henry Miller, American writer

Okay, so you've begun to practise mindfulness, noticing your breathing and maybe even noticing your thoughts and feelings. This now raises a very interesting question: what is this part of you that does all the noticing?

In the classic Buddhist tradition, when you cultivate mindfulness, you also cultivate an awareness process referred to as introspection (Sanskrit: *sampajanna*). You may remember that we introduced this idea in Chapter 2 when we discussed meditation. Introspection is often translated as "clear comprehension" and, according to Buddhist scholar Alan Wallace, it involves "the repeated examination of the state of one's body and mind."[14] You can think of it as operating a bit like a quality-control mechanism that provides continuous feedback to you on how your mindfulness practice is going.

As you practise mindfulness of breathing, for example, introspection is the knack for noticing when your mind has been distracted by thoughts and has lost focus on the breath. Through introspection, you pay attention to your body. You may become aware of the position of you hands, the sensations in your abdomen and the sound of your voice, for example.

This is not simply an exercise of "navel gazing", because as you bring this skill into your everyday life you also become more aware of your environment. In other words, through introspection you notice if your behavior is appropriate or inappropriate to your current circumstances. "Should I smile now?" "Is the content and tone of my voice too harsh, too soft, or just what's needed?" As a form of self-awareness, introspection also operates as an emotional intelligence that continually monitors your feelings, thoughts and actions and their impact on your behavior.

THE OBSERVING SELF

Although cognitive psychology traditionally confines itself to talking about cognitions (thoughts), affects (feelings) and behavior, it also recognizes this distinctly human capability. Psychology uses the term metacognition when referring to this ability to be aware, which means "above" or "beyond thinking". Although slightly broader than the specific Buddhist idea of introspection, it too incorporates this ability to be aware of your experience.

Some psychologists prefer to call this aspect of the mind the "observing self" because it describes more clearly what is actually happening – you are simply observing your experience.[15] Rather than being caught up in thinking about the experience or judging it, your observing self operates like a disinterested spectator.

As aspects of the observing self, mindfulness and introspection work together. And without getting involved in philosophical or metaphysical discussions of the nature of the mind, our experience itself tells us that there are two distinct parts to the mind. The one we're most familiar with is the "thinking self". The thinking self is, well, always thinking. It generates a continuous stream of thoughts in the form of beliefs, memories, judgments, fantasies and plans. It even includes thoughts about your physical "self" – your body.

On the other hand, there's a part of our minds that rises above thinking and simply notices that we are noticing. The "observing self" operates like a viewing platform from which you can view how your mind behaves. It creates the place from which you can observe your experience without getting distracted by all of the mental chatter and emotional turmoil that goes along with being immersed in thinking about your experience.

YOU ALWAYS TAKE THE WEATHER WITH YOU

Although we don't have a good word for it in everyday language, we often recognize it as an experience of pure awareness. We experience pure awareness, for example, when we notice something beautiful in nature. Just recently, I was driving in the countryside after a rain shower and saw a spectacular rainbow. It wasn't long before that awareness was interrupted by the thought, *"Oh, I wish I could stop and take a picture!"* For a brief moment we're not engaged in thinking about the experience, but we are aware of being aware of the experience itself.

Most contemporary Buddhists commonly use the analogy of the sky to describe this aspect of the mind. Your observing self is like the sky. Mental activity, including thoughts and feelings, are like the weather that continually changes. In this analogy, the sky doesn't cling to specific weather conditions, nor try to get rid of "bad" ones; the weather just is. And, in the words of the Australian band, Crowded House, although it's true that "You always take the weather with you," the fact is that no matter what the weather, the sky is always there and can be accessed by rising above the clouds.

SUMMARY

As an aspect of the observing self, introspection is active in all mindfulness practices. It works to improve the quality of your mindfulness by helping create distance from your thoughts and emotions instead of being swept up by them. It's a kind of focused attention that allows you to see the internal working of your own mind as well as the effect of your behavior.

Although the emphasis in introspection is on observing the experience rather than thinking about it, additionally there is a potential therapeutic upside.

The ability to recognize and to "name and explain" the thoughts and emotions you are experiencing also helps to prevent you from being overwhelmed by them. For example, there's a big difference between thinking that you're feeling sad or angry, and recognizing that you're having sad or angry thoughts. The former approach implies that you're closely identified with them, whereas the later approach suggests you are able to detach from them. This potentially opens up greater freedom of choice over your behavior.

In this sense, introspection is a skill that supports greater mindfulness, because it makes it possible to distinguish between having an experience and identifying too closely with it. It really is the gateway to a greater awareness of the workings of your Self, as well as your influence on the world around you.

THE PRACTICE

✓ Check your emotional pulse. Make it a habit to monitor your mental and emotional state through your observing self.

✓ Become a witness to your thoughts and notice physical signs that accompany a particular feeling.

✓ Ask yourself, "Am I at ease in this moment?" or "What is going on inside me at this moment?"

✓ Direct your attention into the body and ask, "Is there any tension?"

✓ Direct your attention to your breathing – notice if it is long or short, fast or slow.

✓ Pay particular attention to other people's emotional reactions to you and consider your behavior in light of this feedback.

✓ Don't give all your attention to the external world; keep some of your attention focused on your inner world.

✓ Observe your mind at work and notice your resistance to simply paying attention without getting involved in thinking or talking about your experience.

✓ Make it a habit to ask yourself, "What's going on inside me right now?"

✓ Notice any moments when your mind becomes still – how do you feel?

CHAPTER 8
THE POWER OF NOW

The secret of health for both mind and body is not to mourn for the past, not to worry about the future, not to anticipate troubles, but to live in the present moment wisely and earnestly.

Buddha

When people think about mindfulness in the popular sense, they usually associate it with "being in the moment" or "being fully present". And it's certainly true that being aware of the present moment lies at the very core of all mindfulness.

Some years ago, before mindfulness become popular in the West, you may remember Eckhart Tolle's book *The Power of Now*, which went on to be an international bestseller.

Tolle drew our attention to something obvious that's always been right in front of us: our life is happening now – in this moment. We can think about the past or the future, but they only exist as thoughts occurring in the present moment. We can plan for the future, but that planning happens here and now. We can reflect on and learn from the past, but that reflection happens in the present. This moment is all we ever have.

WHY IS THIS IMPORTANT?

It's important because, from a psychological perspective, many people tend to live their lives in either the past or the future, or both. We find ourselves caught up in sentiment about the "glory days", sad or regretful about the things we've left behind or the opportunities missed. What's more, all of our opinions are based on what has happened in the past. This makes it difficult to experience things in a fresh, nonjudgmental way in the present.

Equally, we spend a lot of time striving to achieve the future we imagine, or we may feel anxious about the future with all of its uncertainty, worried about the things we can't control. Perhaps Mark Twain said it best when he said, "I have been through some terrible things in my life, some of which actually happened."

It may be that we often don't like the present because the normal state of the thinking mind is in an almost continuous state of low level dis-ease, discontent, boredom or nervousness. We have a tendency to move away from the present moment, either through numbing it or making it more exciting. But by being drawn away from the present moment, we waste time and energy, lose our peace of mind, and also miss the new potential that the present moment offers us.

CLOCK TIME VS. PSYCHOLOGICAL TIME

Of course, this is not to say that people shouldn't plan for the future or learn from past mistakes. In *The Power of Now*, Tolle describes two ways of considering time that I find really helpful. He differentiates between what he calls "clock time" and "psychological time".

We use clock time to organize the practical aspects of our lives, such as setting goals or planning a trip, or even learning from past mistakes so we don't repeat them. But any lesson from the past only becomes relevant when applied in the present. Any planning, as well as working toward achieving a particular goal, is done *now*. So it's important to return immediately to present-moment awareness when those practical matters have been dealt with.

In this way, there will be no build-up of what he calls psychological time. This is the tendency we have to identify too closely with the past and continually project ourselves into an imaginary future.

Of course, this view is immediately compatible with mindfulness. The main focus of attention when we're being mindful is always the present moment. We remain aware of time, but as we practice being mindful, we are increasingly free of psychological time. For example, if you made a mistake in the past and learn from it now, you are using clock time. On the other hand, if you dwell on it and begin criticizing yourself or experiencing remorse or guilt, then you are making the mistake into one of "me" and "mine". That is, you make it part of your sense of Self, and it has become psychological time, which, according to Tolle, is always linked to a false sense of identity.

Through mindfulness, we cultivate a more relaxed "awareness". This enables us to overcome the automatic judgments and limitations of our mind-made sense of Self with its endless stream of thoughts that draw us into the past or project us to the future. Increasingly, as we move off autopilot and become more fully aware of the present moment, the aim is to become a "watcher", an observer of our own thoughts and emotions rather than allowing them to drive our actions and emotions.

Bringing our minds back to observing the present moment is also an effective strategy for overcoming fear, as most fear is rooted in a feeling of loss of control over some imagined future. As the celebrated Russian author Leo Tolstoy once said, "There is only one time that is important – *now*! It is the most important time because it is the only time that we have any power."

To a large degree, our peace of mind is determined by how much power we have to remain fully aware of the present moment. Regardless of what occurred yesterday or in the distant past, and what may or may not happen tomorrow, we are always in the present moment. The only question is to what degree we choose to be present.

Opening up to the full awareness of our experience and bringing a more peaceful mind and renewed purpose to each moment creates what Tolle calls "presence". Presence is necessary to become aware of beauty, to listen with authentic curiosity to someone and share their experience, to be attentive to our own bodies and to observe the flow of our conscious thoughts without being caught up.

To develop "presence" and enhance awareness, the mind needs to be still. Resting the mind in this way feels like putting down a heavy bag full of concerns and worries about the past and future, including judgments and preconceptions. Through this process, we acquire greater self-awareness and self-knowledge, two elements that lie at the core of increasing our emotional intelligence and changing our behavior.

MINDFULNESS AND THE MUNDANE

Of course, being mindful of the present moment isn't only about formal practice or meditation; it's an approach that we bring to normal, even mundane activities such as washing the dishes, taking a shower, sitting in the car, walking up steps, drinking a cup of coffee, and yes, even breathing. Being mindful during all of these activities is about learning to quiet your mind and focus completely on the present experience – being aware of the sensory input, the sounds, the smells, and the feelings associated with that experience.

As you read these words on the page, where is the focus of your attention? Is your mind involved in mental commentary, or anticipating worry or longing for a past experience? Or are you fully aware of the words on the page and their meaning, as well as your surroundings? According to the mindfulness tradition, to find peace of mind and be at ease with yourself, all you need to do is accept this moment fully. Learning to live in the present moment wisely and earnestly is the powerful secret of health for both the mind and body.

THE PRACTICE

✓ Your breath is your always-available anchor to the here and now – tune into it often throughout the day.

✓ Pay attention to your immediate environment and linger on that awareness for a few moments, noticing the sounds, sights and sensations.

✓ When you notice your mind reminiscing about sad feelings or regrets about the past, bring your concentration immediately to the present moment.

✓ Whenever you catch yourself ruminating or feeling anxious about the future, return your attention immediately to the activities in front of you, in the present moment.

✓ When you are eating a meal, notice closely what you are eating and the sensation and pleasure associated with it.

✓ Throughout the day, regularly pause and bring your attention back to the present moment of your experience, observing it silently.

CHAPTER 9
LETTING GO AND
LIGHTENING UP

The first rule is to keep an untroubled spirit. The second is to look things in the face and know them for what they are.
Marcus Aurelius, Roman Emperor and Stoic Philosopher

We've already seen that one of the core elements of mindfulness involves the ability to suspend being judgmental of your circumstances and yourself. In this chapter, we "push the envelope" further and explore the radical implications of applying this central idea to daily life.

According to the tradition behind mindfulness, most of our suffering occurs because of the view we take of our experiences. We have an over exaggerated tendency to hang on tightly to experiences that bring us pleasure, and work very hard to avoid painful experiences. This is normal. But in the mindfulness tradition, both responses constitute "attachment" and are the real source of most of our suffering.

Mindfulness suggests that the way to reduce your suffering is to reduce your degree of attachment both to objects and outcomes. This involves learning to "let go" of your default tendency to pass judgment – "this is good" or "this is bad," "I must have this" or

"I can't stand that." In other words, to live mindfully is to feel emotions, think thoughts and experience life, but without holding tightly to the story that this is how something "should" or "shouldn't" be or continue to be.

TURNING TOWARD EXPERIENCE

Instead, mindfulness practice encourages a willingness to open up to what is occurring in the world within you and around you with a more accepting attitude. Rather than relying on your defences to avoid difficult experiences, mindfulness involves turning toward your experiences with a radical acceptance of reality.

This makes perfect sense from a psychological point of view. Take negative emotions such as anxiety or fear, for example. Both of these generate discomfort and you will feel a strong urge to get rid of them or avoid them. This is understandable, and avoidance is a strategy that works effectively when you are confronted with physical threats. Unfortunately, it fails hopelessly when dealing with psychological challenges like anxiety and fear.

On the contrary, working hard to try to avoid unpleasant thoughts or feelings sets up a painful internal conflict that leaves you vulnerable to greater suffering. When you attempt to avoid difficult thoughts and emotions through suppressing or avoiding them, more often than not this has the effect of amplifying them. Typically this often leaves you vulnerable to obsessive or compulsive behavior.

Mindfulness is not an attempt to distract yourself from difficult content in your mind, not at all. In fact, it's the complete opposite.

Mindfulness offers a more proactive approach by encouraging a less judgmental, more curious, inquisitive strategy. Moving toward the experience and asking yourself, "What is this experience?" has a tendency to moderate the aversion and distress, as well as reduce the emotional gap between what you want and what you've actually got.

Learning to observe feelings and thoughts is the first step. Accepting them as they are, even though painful, is the second step in learning how to reduce the struggle with both the pleasant and unpleasant aspects of our lives.

RIGHT MINDFULNESS AND RIGHT ACTION

Let's be clear, though, this is not about trying to maintain some phony "happy state" or about denying emotional pain. Neither does it imply a passive resignation – a "grit your teeth and bear it" approach. And it certainly doesn't mean a passive submission to your circumstances.

On the contrary, the ancient tradition within which mindfulness is embedded makes it crystal clear that mindfulness involves a commitment to an ethical lifestyle. We'll discuss this in more detail in the next chapter. For now, it's important to note that mindfulness is not as passive or as disinterested as many people teach in popular courses.

Right mindfulness involves taking action that is in line with your deepest-held values. For example, if you witnessed injustice or were in an abusive relationship, being mindful involves making room for the painful thoughts and feelings rather than simply reacting to them. Instead of dealing with your anger through destructive "acting out" or with self-defeating behavior such as excessive drinking or passive submission, acting mindfully involves finding ways to improve the situation according to your values.

In other words, acceptance in the mindfulness tradition is more about accepting your personal experiences – thoughts, feelings and memories – rather than passively accepting the circumstances of your life. It's about actively making room for unwanted thoughts and feelings, memories and sensations that you normally work hard to avoid. Interestingly, the Latin word for "acceptance" is *capere*, which literally means "take". When we accept something we "take what is offered".

ACCEPTANCE, SEPARATION AND FREEDOM

This brings us to a most important insight. In mindfulness, the actual content of the thought or emotion is not considered to be the real problem; it's only when you identify closely with these experiences that problems arise. While you are entangled with the thoughts and difficult experiences, you fail to notice how much they control you.

So, by being fully present in the moment, stepping back from the brink of your reaction and using the observing self, you are able to notice the relationship that links thoughts and emotions to your predictable actions as they occur. In this way, mindfulness is an approach that undermines your habitual need to be in control – that is, trying to control your thoughts and feelings – rather than creating the psychological space for acceptance of them.

Once you can create the psychological space through greater acceptance of your experience, you are able to reduce the potential negative gravitational pull of states such as depressed mood or anxiety. So, rather than life being dominated by working hard to avoid such negative states, taking a more accepting approach opens up greater freedom to choose behavior aligned with your values and the outcomes you want to achieve. We will take up this theme and explore it further in the next chapter and then again in Chapter 17.

THE PRACTICE

✓ Make peace with imperfection. Whenever we are too attached to having something a certain way, we set up the conditions for inner conflict.

✓ No matter what happened yesterday or what may happen tomorrow, learn to live in the present moment.

✓ Develop more patience and add an element of ease and acceptance to your life.

✓ Establish patience periods, when for five minutes at a time you decide not to let anything disturb your peace of mind.

✓ Accept the fact that life isn't fair.

✓ See the glass as already broken. This Buddhist teaching reminds us that life is in a constant state of change. Everything has a beginning and an end.

✓ Notice your moods and don't make important choices when your mood is low.

✓ Let go of your expectations and lighten up. You're more likely to be surprised by joy.

✓ Surrender to the present moment and allow it to be okay the way it is for the moment.

✓ Take a long, deep, mindful breath and soften your response.

CHAPTER 10
FINDING WHAT YOU CARE ABOUT

Let everything you do be done as if it makes a difference. It does.
William James

To many people, the initial attraction of mindfulness is often as a stress-reduction technique. The ability to clarify the mind and relax the body, as a way to relieve stress, is compelling. But I would go further and argue that this is an altogether too limited view of the potential value of mindfulness practice.

In a genuine effort to distance the secular practice of mindfulness from its original role in nearly all religions, secular trainers often forget that the core of mindfulness is the cultivation of the mind's potential. Beyond the popular emphasis on mindfulness as a purely psychological technique, at its root it is an ethical and spiritual practice. And, of course, by spiritual I don't mean religious. The ultimate aim of mindfulness practice is to assist you to live a more satisfying and personally meaningful life.

As we have seen, mindfulness originates within a tradition that views it as a path to personal liberation. According to Alan Wallace (an expert on Buddhism), "It begins with ethics: treating each other with kindness and doing our best not to cause harm ... Upon the basis of an ethical lifestyle, the path continues with right effort, right mindfulness and right concentration."[16]

The practice of mindfulness, therefore, has implications beyond simply paying attention to the present moment deliberately and non-judgmentally. It can be viewed as involving both ethical commitments and as a psychological practice that fosters personal transformation. Living mindfully and turning inward to practice meditation make us more aware of our own thoughts and actions and, in particular, how our behavior impacts other people. To understand how this works, we need to consider a core idea within mindfulness that challenges the assumption inherent in some of the most popular models of psychology.

MINDFULNESS AND HUMAN POTENTIAL

Most models of psychology operate on the assumption that your thoughts or "self-structures" are somehow "dysfunctional" or "pathological" and need to be fixed or repaired in some way. In fact, the long history of psychology has been preoccupied with human dysfunction in one form or another. But even at the outset of the modern science of psychology, one of its founders, William James, challenged this exclusive preoccupation with human dysfunction and asked what if the average person – even if enjoying sound mental health – were only living up to a fraction of his or her potential?

Of course, more than 100 years later, this question has been picked up and addressed systematically by the movement known as positive psychology. Described by its founding father, Martin Seligman, as "a psychology of positive human functioning," positive psychology focuses not simply on minimizing psychopathology, but on maximizing human potential.

The psychological model underpinning mindfulness also challenges this emphasis on human dysfunction and proposes quite a different approach to achieving personal transformation.

KNOW YOURSELF ... CHANGE YOURSELF

The psychology behind mindfulness does not view the Self as broken and in need of repair. Instead, the psychology of mindfulness proposes that growth and therapeutic change occur through changing your relationship to the idea you have of your Self and your values.

For example, one senior manager in a large organization whom I worked with had for years operated like a tyrant, intimidating his staff. Over the course of mindfulness training, I encouraged him to take a step back and observe himself, in the present moment, without judging himself.

He came to understand that the real force driving his habitual behavior was not malevolence toward his staff at all. Rather, his toxic style was driven by his fear of a loss of control. He also recognized that his management style was incongruent with the view he had of himself and a core value that he held, which was treating others with respect.

Accordingly, as he gained clarity about how he wanted to behave, according to his value of respecting others, he was able to make a shift in his behavior and align his actions with a new understanding of his true Self. Of course, it also dawned on him that his professional success depended on him having an engaged and innovative team, and that his management style had been counterproductive in achieving this, i.e., it wasn't working for him!

In this example, you can see the overlap and interplay between the various elements of mindfulness and how they work together – the observing self and introspection, i.e., coming to know your Self, awareness of the present moment, non-judgmental acceptance of your experience and recognition of your values. All elements of the practice combine, leading to increased self-knowing, psychological flexibility and values-based action.

MINDFULNESS AND VALUES-BASED ACTION

Living according to your values is important in achieving a peaceful mind and living a meaningful life. Values define the relationship you want to have with yourself and the world. They are the core principles that guide your behavior and motivate your choices.

Living mindfully, then, begins with embracing the values of non-judgmental self-acceptance and compassion. It involves the decision to be on good terms with yourself and with others whenever possible. This decision to be on good terms with yourself involves treating yourself kindly and with integrity. In this way, ethical action and living accordingly to core values – the things you care about – not only generate a more peaceful mind, but also a more compassionate approach toward others.

In my book *Emotional Capitalists: The Ultimate Guide for Building Emotional Intelligence for Leaders*,[17] I describe eight valued domains of experience into which we all invest time and emotional energy to achieve emotional balance. We each make decisions about what we care about in the domains of our physical health, lifestyle, self-development, creative expression, work, finances, social relationships and intimate relationships.

Ultimately, emotional balance comes from identifying your core values in each of these domains and living congruently with them. Thus, instead of your behavior being pushed and pulled by competing external demands, including the behavior of others, you operate out of internal reference points that reflect your core values. And while perfect balance is elusive, living more mindfully involves taking ethical action to live in greater accord with your core values.

Some time ago I was coaching a very wealthy banker who worked excessively long hours. Typically he would leave the house at 6am each morning and return after 8pm each evening. I asked him how he would describe himself and his core values. "I'm a family man!" he insisted. I pointed out that he had four children under seven years old and that a "family man", particularly one not constrained by financial need, is more likely to be someone who is there to have breakfast with his kids or at least there to tuck them into bed at night. As he thought about it, it dawned on him that he was not living according to his cherished values at all. Instead, he was operating out of an old script that had guided his sense of identity when he was much younger; one that he'd never updated.

Values reflect the things that are most important to us. They define the way we want to relate to the world, to other people and to ourselves. Ultimately, they're what we want to be known for and guide how we want to behave. For example, your values in the social dimension of your life may include treating others with respect or being cooperative. In the financial dimension, you may value being generous or making a contribution. In the lifestyle dimension, you may value the environment and therefore make choices based on a greater environmental consciousness, and so on.

To live more mindfully is to ask yourself questions such as: "Are you living the life you want to live right now? Is your behavior in each domain of life aligned with your values – the things that are most meaningful to you?"

According to all the wisdom traditions, genuine happiness and peace of mind are achieved by cultivating emotional balance. And, as we'll discover in Part Four, the Four Applications of Mindfulness provide us with a reliable "how-to" set of practices for achieving a more balanced and healthy mind.

In the meantime, use "The Practice" section on this page and the following pages to identify your core values – the things you care about in each dimension of your life. Ask yourself: "What's my value here? Are the choices I'm making aligned with my values?"

THE PRACTICE

✓ **Social Relationships**: Imagine your interpersonal relationships. How do you come across to others? What values guide the development of your reputation?

✓ **Intimate Relationships**: Describe your relationships with your close friends, family and children. How do you relate to the people who are closest to you? What values guide your behavior?

✓ **Health**: Imagine yourself in the near future as the picture of health. Notice how you look. Notice your weight and energy levels. How do you exercise? What values govern your choices of what you eat? What values guide the good habits you have incorporated into your life in this domain?

✓ **Lifestyle**: Visualise your ideal lifestyle in the near future. How do you handle your time? Where do you live? What's the level of stressful activity in your life? What values guide your choices?

✓ **Self-Development**: Picture yourself in the near future, developing yourself to your maximum potential. What qualities, attitudes and emotions do you include or eliminate from your character? What spiritual qualities or strengths have you developed? What new knowledge or skills have you learned?

✓ **Creative Expression**: Describe what your unique creative expression looks like. How do you express it? Is it through music, dance, poetry, hobbies, collections, or art and crafts? Perhaps it's through writing, sculpting, gardening or decorating? What values guide your decisions?

✓ **Career**: Think of the career in which you are engaged in the near future. See your responsibilities, the environments you work in, and the accomplishments you've achieved. What values guide you toward achieving the satisfaction that you get from your work?

✓ **Finance**: Imagine what you want your financial status to be in the near future. How do you relate to money? How do you spend it? What values guide how you use your financial resources?

PART THREE

FOUR APPLICATIONS OF MINDFULNESS

CHAPTER 11
MINDFULNESS
OF THE BODY

An emotion is your body's reaction to your mind.

Eckhart Tolle, author

There is more wisdom in your body than in your deepest philosophies.

Friedrich Nietzche, philosopher and poet

As a clinical psychologist, I'm very interested in mental health and the relationship between the mind and the body and, in particular, how psychological mechanisms can exert powerful influence over the body and vice versa. Interestingly, in the nine years I spent at various graduate schools training to be a clinical psychologist, I learned very little about the connection between the mind and the body.

I learned about how thoughts direct feelings. I learned about mental disorders and the suffering they create, and I even learned about positive psychology and the importance of developing an optimistic perspective. However, I heard very little about the way the body influences the mind or about the importance of the body as a vehicle to connect to the mind.

I heard nothing, for example, about how the breath could be used to influence the autonomic nervous system, control anxiety and regulate mental states (a theme explored in Chapter 15). Nor did I learn anything about the role the body plays in altering states of consciousness and creating the conditions for the mind to perform at its best.

Fortunately, today medical science and clinical psychology are more receptive to an integrative approach to health and wellbeing. Both disciplines recognize that what happens in your body affects what goes on in your mind and vice versa.

THE BODY HAS A MIND OF ITS OWN

As an approach to training the mind, mindfulness practice almost always begins by directing your attention to the body. This includes the sense fields such as seeing, hearing, touching, tasting and smelling. These senses also act as a doorway to greater awareness of your immediate physical environment.

We sometimes say that the body has a mind of its own. The French philosopher Michel de Montaigne, for example, noted how our facial expressions betray our secret thoughts; our hair stands on end, our hearts race, and our bowels and anal sphincters undergo "dilations and contractions proper to [themselves], independent of our wishes or even opposed to them."[18] Of course, we now know that many of these effects are controlled by the autonomic nervous system, over which we have very limited voluntary control. The body represents a powerful instrument for accessing and influencing our state of mind and is worth paying closer attention to for at least three important reasons.

1. THE UNITY OF MIND AND BODY

At the most fundamental level, your body is critical to your physical and emotional health and wellbeing. With busy and demanding lives, we often spend so much time "in our heads" that it's easy to neglect the care of our bodies. Poor nutrition, lack of exercise, insufficient sleep, or worse, destructive habits such as, well ... you don't need me to name them! These all take a toll on your mental and physical health and wellbeing. This tendency to disregard the body can also be reinforced by holding critical views of your body. In fact, many people only seem to pay careful attention to their bodies when they experience pain, dysfunction or pleasure.

Becoming more mindful of your body draws your attention to the fact that you are an embodied being – that your mind and body are one. To view the body as secondary in importance to your mind is at odds with your physiology and sets up the potential for dis-ease.

2. YOUR EARLY WARNING SYSTEM

The autonomic nervous system does not necessarily differentiate between different causes of arousal, such as physical pain, or emotional states, such as worry and anger, or nervous excitement. All of these experiences might result in fairly similar bodily sensations. Obviously, you can usually notice the difference between the body sensations of arousal, such as increased heart rate, faster breathing, tension, anxiety, nervousness or panic, and the body sensations associated with relaxation and calmness. But the body often detects your emotions and thoughts before you've consciously noticed them. For example, we can become aware of tightness in the chest or a clenched jaw before we notice that we feel angry.

Similarly, we notice blushing before being aware that we feel self-conscious or embarrassed.

Practicing a more mindful approach to your body encourages you to pay attention to your physical experience in a non-judgmental, emotionally neutral way, irrespective of whether your experience is pleasant or unpleasant. Observing your bodily experience non-judgmentally helps you gain early insight into the nature of what's underlying the emotional or conceptual content of your experience. This provides you with a greater opportunity to develop a different relationship to your experience.

Think of mindfulness of the body as an early-detection system that can provide you with greater opportunity to *respond* rather than *react* to your circumstances. Psychologist Paul Ekman describes this experience as the "space between the spark and the flame." What Paul means is that the earlier you detect the spark of a feeling such as anger in your physiology (perhaps through noticing increased heart rate and tightness in the chest), the better the chance you have of interrupting your automatic reaction before it becomes a flame of destructive behavior.

3. TUNE IN TO THE BODY TO TUNE OUT THE MIND

There's another really good reason why paying greater attention to the body helps you develop a more peaceful mind. Neuroscience has established that some parts of the brain are linked by something called "reciprocal inhibition"; that is, activity in one part of the brain inhibits activity in another part of the brain. According to neuroscientists Rick Hanson and Richard Mendius, different parts of the left and right hemispheres operate like this to some extent.

When you stimulate areas of the right hemisphere by engaging the activities it specializes in, such as making you aware of the state of your body, the verbal centres of the left hemisphere responsible for verbal chatter are effectively silenced.[19]

In this sense, you can use mindfulness of the body as an anchor when the mind is caught up in what neuroscientist Norman Farb has described as "narrative mode". Imagine you're enjoying a Sunday morning walk in the park. Instead of enjoying your surroundings and the leisure of having no particular immediate demands on your time, you find yourself ruminating about a meeting you have to present at the following week. Your mind begins to prepare a story about how that's likely to turn out.

By shifting your attention into "experiential mode", where you focus instead on the bodily sensations of the warmth of the sun on your face and the fresh breeze brushing your hair, or to the sound of birdsong around you, the narrative neural circuitry is reduced. Farb's research has shown that people who practice mindfulness of the body, at the very least, develop stronger capacities to notice the difference between the narrative and experiential modes. But what's more exciting is that they are able to switch more easily between these modes. Accordingly, mindfulness of the body gives us an effective anchor to ground our experience and manage our moods more effectively.

THE BODY SCAN

To practice mindfulness of the body, as usual, start with the breath as a whole, noting the sensations of your breath in your abdomen, chest, throat and nose. Then allow your attention to move systematically from sensation to sensation throughout your body. Use the brief body scan exercise described in "The Practice" section to guide you, or download *The Body Scan Meditation* MP3 from the website for a more detailed guided meditation.

THE PRACTICE

The Body Scan Meditation

In this session, we deepen our experience of relaxation and cultivate greater familiarity with our bodily experiences through the body scan technique. This practice involves scanning the body by moving attention around the body, pausing and holding attention on each region for a few minutes.

Once again, settle yourself into a comfortable position, either sitting on a chair or cushion or lying on a mat. Settle yourself into whatever posture you have chosen. Let your eyes close.

Allow your awareness to descend into the entire field of the body ... begin by simply becoming aware of the physical sensations as you experience them in your body. Let all the muscles of your body become loose and limp. Let go.

As the body relaxes and the mind becomes calmer, imagine that your field of awareness is like a spotlight, and bring it to your feet, focusing specifically on the sensation in your feet.

Simply observe whatever tactile sensations, if any, you feel in that area.

Now bring your attention up your left and right legs, noticing any tightness or sensations. Bring your awareness up into the buttocks and become aware of your pelvic region and hips.

Move your attention to the lower torso, the lower abdomen and lower back, noticing any sensations occurring there, particularly any sensations of movement associated with the breathing.

Move up to the diaphragm, the bottom of the rib cage, and at the very centre focus on the solar plexus and the chest. Feel your rib cage rising and falling as you breathe gently. Now move your attention through the chest to your upper back.

Move your awareness to your shoulders and down your arms.

Now focus on your neck. Then continue up the back of the head to the crown.

Now move your awareness to your forehead, down to the level of the eyes and the nose, across the cheeks, and down to the mouth and the chin. Slightly expand the field to cover your whole face and notice your lips. Take your time to be mindful of your entire head, opening up to the physical sensations as you experience them.

Very briefly, return to the crown of the head. Taking only a few seconds, rapidly scan from the top of the head down to the tips of the toes. Now come back to the crown of the head, and for a second time, taking just a few seconds, sweep all the way through the body. Then, for a third and final time, come to the crown of the head and sweep through the body. Feel the breath sweeping up and down your body and get a sense of your body as a whole.

Expand your awareness to include simultaneously the entire field of tactile sensation, from the crown of your head to the base of your thighs and to the tips of your toes. Attend to these sensations closely.

Slowly open your eyes. Without breaking focus, direct the same quality of awareness, this stillness and bare attention, to the visual domain of experience. Note what you see – colours and shapes.

CHAPTER 12
MINDFULNESS OF THOUGHTS AND FEELINGS

That all is as thinking makes it so – and you control your thinking. So remove your judgments whenever you wish and then there is calm – as the sailor rounding the cape finds smooth water and the welcome of a waveless bay.

Marcus Aurelius, Roman Emperor and Stoic Philosopher

In the previous chapter, we discovered that becoming more mindful of our bodies invariably leads to becoming more aware of what's going on in our minds. In this chapter, we consider how mindfulness of feelings and thoughts helps us develop greater psychological flexibility and reduce our suffering.

IF IT AIN'T BROKE, DON'T FIX IT

As I suggested in Chapter 10, most models of Western psychology operate on the assumption that human beings are essentially damaged, and that troubling thoughts and feelings are viewed as a form of psychopathology that result in dysfunctional behavior. "Fixing" damaged or disordered thinking, therefore, is the primary route to changing behavior. Accordingly, Western systems of psychotherapy tend to focus on techniques to reduce symptoms by challenging and replacing faulty, disordered thought processes with more rational ones.

Now, it is true that our minds have a natural tendency to become destructive quite easily. Generally we experience negative feelings more intensely and more readily than positive ones. Even on the happiest days of our lives, we can relive painful memories or get lost in fearful predictions of the future. Recently, during one of those happy days, I attended my daughter's wedding. During the ceremony, I was suddenly struck by a feeling of profound sadness at the thought, "What if they break up in the future?"

We're all the same. No matter how privileged our lives may be, we are all vulnerable to thoughts and feelings that create pain, along with the dysfunctional behavioral responses they generate.

As we saw in Chapter 6, the psychology behind mindfulness operates on a radically different assumption about the Self. Instead of seeing the Self, with all its thoughts and feelings, as broken and therefore in need of being "fixed", the psychology behind mindfulness challenges the idea that the Self exists as an independent, permanent entity. So, if it ain't broke, don't fix it. Rather than try and fix something that doesn't really exist objectively, the objective of mindfulness is to change the nature of the relationship you have to the thoughts and feelings that create your experience.

ATTACHMENT AND AVERSION

Eastern psychology identifies two normal processes of the mind that are at the root of all emotional pain. The first is attachment – the tendency to attach closely to pleasant thoughts and feelings, trying to hold on to them forever. The second process is avoidance – the inclination to push away what we don't like, trying to avoid it at all costs.

In relation to the strategy of avoidance, Harvard psychologist Daniel Wegner's research is enlightening. Wegner noticed an obscure but intriguing quote from Dostoyevsky's *Winter Notes on Summer Impressions*: "Try to pose for yourself this task: not to think of a polar bear, and you will see that the cursed thing will come to mind every minute." Wegner set up experiments in which he asked volunteers to sit alone in a room and told them to think about anything, but not to imagine Dostoyevsky's white bear. Results showed that suppression of the unwanted thought led to a rebound effect that increased both the intensity and frequency of the unwanted thought.

According to the mindfulness tradition, both the process of desperately trying to avoid some experiences or attaching tightly to others result in increasing our vulnerability to emotional pain. Pain is an inevitable part of human experience, but the intense *suffering* we experience is an optional extra, generated from attachment to our experience and the judgments we make about it.

To live mindfully is to feel emotions, think thoughts and experience life, but without becoming overly identified with the mental narratives about how something "should" or "should not" be. To achieve a more peaceful mind, it is necessary to learn how to stop trying to fix things – to stop being so worried about trying to control your experience of external realities and to stop trying to replace disagreeable thoughts with more agreeable ones.

VIEW THOUGHTS AND FEELINGS AS MENTAL EVENTS

Okay, so if it's not possible to stop thinking, your next step is to begin noticing your thoughts as they occur in real time. Through the practice of mindfulness of thoughts and feelings, your aim is simply to observe and view thoughts and feelings as mental events in the same way you might view external events, such as the weather.

It seems obvious, but it's important to realize that you are constantly thinking. In fact, it's so obvious that you're sometimes misled into believing that you are already aware of this fact. Think, for a moment, about your breathing. Chances are that until I drew your attention to it, you were not conscious that you were doing it. Unless you experience something that prevents you from breathing, you simply forget that you're doing it.

It's the same with thinking. Because it happens automatically, it's easy to forget that you're doing it, and you fail to notice it. In contrast to breathing, however, not being aware of what you are thinking can lead to a lot of emotional pain. There's a direct correlation between the content of your thoughts and the emotions you experience as painful feelings. Try getting anxious, for example, without first having anxious thoughts!

A TALE OF TWO DARTS ... OUCH!

Some physical pain is inescapable; it acts as a warning system so that we avoid danger. In the mindfulness tradition, it is sometimes referred to as the "first dart" of existence. The first dart represents the suffering that all of us experience simply because we are human. Life is a source of pain in the sense that distressing and unwelcomed physical and emotional experiences occur. These experiences, however, are often made far worse by our reactions to them, and it's these reactions that the mindfulness tradition refers to as "second darts".

At the risk of trivializing the profound existential value of this insight, let me illustrate. I recently had the experience of getting up in the middle of the night and stepped on a piece of Lego buried in the shag carpet. Now trust me, that was a first-dart experience! But my distressed, angry reaction, "Who left the bloody Lego out?" was definitely a second-dart experience. First darts are unpleasant, to be sure, but our suffering is compounded by second-dart reactions. Mindfulness of thoughts and feelings makes us acutely aware that our second-dart reactions are optional; they are the darts we throw at other people, as well as ourselves.

Of course, this is profoundly true of our broad human experience. Often we experience things we don't want. And even when we do get what we want, we can't keep them forever. When we react by working hard to avoid the experience or, instead, by obsessively clinging to the experience, we add levels of unnecessary pain. Instead, mindfulness makes us aware of the thoughts and feelings associated with the experience without necessarily allowing them to escalate into a cascade of second-dart reactions.

This by no means suggests that getting excited or becoming passionate about life, or even getting angry about injustice, are somehow antithetical to being mindful – not at all. Second darts become a problem when they become a default setting leading to a constant state of moderate to high arousal and stress. For all the effects on the body that we'll discuss in Chapter 15, second darts typically have their most damaging impact on our emotional wellbeing.

PRACTICE MINDFULNESS OF THOUGHTS AND FEELINGS

To practice mindfulness of thoughts and feelings, as usual, start with the breath as a whole, noting the sensations of the breath in your abdomen, chest, throat and nose. Then allow your attention to move systematically from sensation to sensation, throughout your body. Use the brief *Mindfulness of Thoughts and Feelings Meditation* described in the "The Practice" section to guide you, or download the more extended *Mindfulness of Thoughts and Feelings Meditation* MP3 from the website for the guided version.

THE PRACTICE

Mindfulness of Thoughts and Feelings Meditation
Settle yourself into a comfortable position, either sitting on a chair or cushion or lying on a mat. Keep your abdominal muscles loose, so that when you breathe you can feel the breath go right down to the abdomen and feel your abdomen expand with each inhalation. Keep your shoulders relaxed and hands resting comfortably in your lap or at your sides.

Allow your eyes to close or, if you prefer, leave your eyes partially open and simply lower your gaze, unfocused on an area in front of you.

Let all the muscles of your body become loose and limp, and settle your body into a posture of ease and comfort.

Now bring your awareness more directly to the breath as it moves in and out of the body. And without trying to control your breathing in any way, let your breath find its own natural rhythm, like waves crashing on the seashore.

Let your body remain completely still, like a mountain.

Elevate your awareness to the space of the mind and imagine your mind as vast as space itself. Focus your attention on this mental space and observe the vast emptiness. You can imagine this space as if it's a screen at the cinema. You just sit watching, waiting for a thought to arrive. When it does, just attend to it as if it's "on the screen". Notice any thoughts that you may be having. Are they thoughts about the future or the past?

Observe them as mental events of the mind without getting caught up in them or chasing them; just watch them for a moment and let them go. Let them dissolve or watch them blow away like a cloud and refocus on the space of the mind.

No matter what arrives within this mental space, a thought or image, perhaps an emotion or a feeling, simply attend to it and observe it without reacting to it or engaging with it. Just let thoughts come and go on their own.

It's quite natural to get caught up in thoughts and carried away. With your faculty of introspection, notice when you get caught up with a thought, perhaps caught up in the drama on screen. When you become aware of this, simply relax, return to your seat and observe the empty screen of your mind once again. If any thoughts evoke intense emotions, either pleasant or unpleasant, as best you can just simply note the feelings and let them be.

Now focus on the interval between thoughts, the vast emptiness of the mind from which thoughts emerge and into which they dissolve.

Remember, if at any time you become aware that your mind has become unfocused or spaced out, or if you find your mind repeatedly drawn into the story of your thoughts, you can always come back to mindfulness of the breath and become aware of your whole body; just sit and breathe and restabilize your attention back to the present moment.

Finish the session by taking three long, slow, deep breaths. Finally, breathing out, effortlessly release the breath – mindfully attentive to the sensations throughout the body.

Now allow your eyes to open and become fully aware of your surroundings and notice how you feel.

CHAPTER 13
MINDFULNESS AND EMOTIONAL INTELLIGENCE

Between stimulus and response, there is a space. In that space is our power to choose our response. In our response lies our growth and our freedom.

Victor Frankl, neurologist and psychiatrist

Every now and again, ideas come along that really do change the world. Emotional Intelligence is one of those ideas that has changed most of what we thought we knew about how people process information, make decisions, manage stress, innovate, lead, and influence other people effectively.

The idea of emotional intelligence has a long research-based history, but became popular in 1995 when American journalist Daniel Goleman wrote the first best-selling book on the subject. One of the best definitions of emotional intelligence, though, actually comes from the two scholars who first described the theoretical framework, John D. Mayer and Peter Salovey:

The ability to monitor one's own and others' feelings and emotions, to discriminate among them, and to use this information to guide one's thinking and actions.[20]

According to this definition, emotional intelligence essentially involves two abilities: first, becoming aware of how emotions in others and ourselves support behavior, and second, developing the skills to manage these emotions intelligently to solve problems that are emotionally and socially based.

Since Goleman published *Emotional Intelligence* nearly 20 years ago, our own research over the last decade or so using the *Emotional Capital Report*™ (ECR) has validated these claims on a global scale.[21] And the Emotional Capital model also fits with Goleman's more recent writings about mindfulness and the need to train attention in three areas – what he calls a "triple focus".

INNER FOCUS – SELF-KNOWING AND SELF-CONTROL

In Goleman's *triple focus* model, the first area includes an *inner* focus. This involves developing greater self-awareness. Self-awareness is essentially the foundation upon which emotional intelligence is built, as it forms a platform for understanding and developing all other competencies in the model.

In our approach to working with emotional intelligence, we begin with mindfulness, because at the core of emotional intelligence is the ability to monitor your own feelings and emotions.

Beginning with mindfulness, however, actually moves us beyond self-awareness, because it leads to greater self-knowledge. So in our model we refer to self-awareness as self-knowing. And as we saw in Chapters 11 and 12, awareness of your emotions begins with paying attention to the subtle physiological reactions in the body and continues with cultivating an ability to observe your thoughts and emotions objectively and non-judgmentally. Accurately decoding these internal cues from your body and mind holds the key to emotionally intelligent behavior.

According to Goleman, "The brain harbours our deepest sense of purpose and meaning in ... subcortical regions – areas connected poorly to the verbal areas of the neocortex, but richly to the gut. We know our values by first getting a visceral sense of what feels right and what does not, then articulating those feelings for ourselves."[22] Self-knowing, then, depends on being able to see yourself objectively. This requires the ability to examine your thoughts and emotions from a third-person perspective, not getting swept up in the emotion, not identifying with it, but just seeing it clearly and objectively. The stable, clear, non-judgmental attention developed through mindfulness provides you with the best possible technology to acquire this insight.

SELF-CONTROL: ENTERING THE GAP BETWEEN THE SPARK AND THE FLAME

Of course, the ability to notice your emotions and manage them well, so that they do not sweep you up, involves a second element of emotional intelligence: self-control. Solid self-control is the skill that enables you to stay calm in a crisis, manage your anxiety and rebound from setbacks.

Some years ago I had a client who was a flight attendant. She'd been referred to me by the courts in Australia for an incident in which she'd attacked a passenger with a bottle of wine. It turned out that she had a long history of impulsive behavior that had led to many angry incidents, but nothing quite as dramatic (or career defining!) as on this occasion.

Over the years, she had received help from counsellors and had managed to gain some control over her behavior, particularly by catching her angry thoughts before they erupted into destructive actions. But all too often, by the time she realized how angry she actually was, it was too late and she ended up regretting her actions.

I used mindfulness of the body to help her recognize her anger as it correlated with sensations in her body. She began to notice, for example, that prior to an incident her breathing became shallow and rapid very quickly and that she clenched her teeth forcefully. She came to recognize these phenomena as very early warning signs of anger arising rapidly. That knowledge gave her the possibility of acting quickly to move away from potentially destructive impulsive responses before they erupted. This is a classic example of Ekman's "spark and flame" idea referred to earlier.

Beyond its function in impulse control, it's hard to overstate how important the emotional skill of self-control is in living a meaningful and successful life. Self-control is the skill that ultimately develops into willpower and self-discipline and enables us to manage our disturbing feelings so we can stay focused on the goals that are important to us. In fact, ever since that remarkable study involving marshmallows and pre-schoolers conducted by Walter Mischel back in the 1960s, decades of research have demonstrated how important it is in determining the course of our lives.[23]

By now, most people have heard of the legendary "marshmallow test". Psychologist Walter Mischel invited pre-schoolers at Stanford

University's Bing Nursery School to play a game. In the room each child was shown a tray with marshmallows or other treats and offered the choice of having one immediately or two if they waited alone for 20 minutes. About a third of the children grabbed and ate the marshmallow immediately, another third held out for a few minutes, and a third managed to wait for the entire 20 minutes. What the pre-schoolers did as they tried to wait unexpectedly turned out to predict a lot about their future lives. The more seconds they waited at age four or five went on to predict stronger academic performance, better self-worth in later life, and greater capacity to cope adaptively with frustration and stress. As Goleman later commented, "Self-control ... is the 'master aptitude' underlying emotional intelligence, essential for constructing a fulfilling life."

OTHER FOCUS – EMPATHY

A second core area of focus in emotional intelligence involves monitoring the feelings and experiences of *other* people. This provides the foundation for emotional skills such as empathy and relationship skills.

Of course, it makes sense that you need to have some insight into your own feelings and experiences before you can possibly understand the feelings and experiences of other people. It's therefore not surprising that, in general, when people score low on the self-knowing scale of the ECR, they also score low on the empathy scale. And empathy is not as psychologically soft as some people imagine.

Essentially, it involves paying mindful attention both to the very concrete reality that someone else describes, as well as grasping the emotional dimensions of their experience, including what they may need from you.

Some years ago, Heinz Kohut, one of Europe's most influential psychoanalysts, suggested that, at the psychological level, people have two essential needs: to be understood and to be admired; however, the most fundamental need is to be understood. Empathy allows you to understand not just what people are facing and feeling, but also what they need from you. It's what we all want from our most important relationships – to be understood. When people feel understood, they are more comfortable sharing their thoughts, feelings and ideas.

Empathy actually has its origin in compassion, which literally means "to feel with". In the end, it's empathy and compassion that connect you with people and enable you to establish valuable connections and effective relationships.

OUTER FOCUS – THE BIG PICTURE

The third area of focus in emotional intelligence involves an *outer* focus. Having applied mindfulness to the body, thoughts and feelings, and even to monitoring the experience of others, the final application is to pay wide-open attention to the broader interrelationships occurring in the world around us. In the classic mindfulness tradition, this application of mindfulness involves paying attention to the patterns of how things work together – because *this* happened, then *that* happened or didn't happen.

From the perspective of emotional intelligence, this involves skills such as optimism, by which we choose to focus on the bigger picture with a genuine sense of the opportunities and possibilities available. Cynics often dismiss optimism as false hope or a lack of realism. But, far from being naïve or having a Pollyanna-ish view of the world, optimists have a particular way of seeing reality, what psychologists call an "explanatory style".

They see problems as temporary, controllable and linked to a specific situation, rather than permanent and intractable. Perhaps Melinda Gates captured the strength of this perspective best in a recent commencement address delivered to Stanford graduates. After visiting a TB hospital in Soweto, where the Bill and Melinda Gates Foundation was working to supply the technology to increase survival rates, she commented: "Optimism for me isn't a passive expectation that things will get better; it's a conviction that we can make things better – that whatever suffering we see, no matter how bad it is, we can help people if we don't lose hope and we don't look away."

For an optimist, it makes no sense to look away. We can always do better, limit the damage, find an alternative solution and rebuild what has been destroyed. Through mindfulness, we become aware of and accept the facts, but then quickly identify the lessons to be learned and the positive opportunities to be grasped.

There is a second emotional skill at work here in this perspective: adaptability. As we have seen, mindfulness involves a flexibility of attention, but this also leads to a flexibility of mind here – an openness to change, an enthusiasm for what's new. By focusing on the outer world and bringing a mindfulness-based emotional intelligence, we come to discover future possibilities and have fun doing it.

THE PRACTICE

✓ When you turn inward to examine yourself, whatever you find, don't judge it, but learn to observe it and even like it.

✓ When experiencing pain or failure, instead of being stridently self-critical, treat yourself with the same kindness and understanding as you would others.

✓ Respond rather than react to difficult situations by introducing a pause before speaking and acting impulsively.

✓ Take the time to pause and give adequate thought to the impact of your words and actions on others.

✓ When tempted to lose control, ask yourself, "Who or what am I trying to control that is beyond my ability to control?" Then focus on what you can control – your actions.

✓ When speaking with people, give them your full attention and the airtime they need.

✓ Listen for the content of what people say as well as the connotation (the emotional implications).

✓ View your problems as temporary, controllable and linked to a specific situation, then look forward and make a commitment to do what it takes to improve the situation, if only marginally.

CHAPTER 14
MINDFULNESS
AND HAPPINESS

The mind is its own place, and in itself can make a heaven of hell or a hell of heaven.

John Milton, Paradise Lost

All joy in this world comes from wanting others to be happy, and all suffering in this world comes from wanting only oneself to be happy.
Shantideva, 8th-century Indian Buddhist monk and scholar

So far in part three we've explored the applications of mindfulness for creating greater awareness of our physical and mental experience with a view to spending less time in "narrative mode" and more time in "experiential mode". In this way, we become more conscious of how thoughts and bodily sensations influence our behavior. We've also seen that through acquiring greater self-knowledge and self-control, we can build our emotional intelligence to help solve some of our emotional and social problems and create greater psychological flexibility. In this chapter, we consider the ultimate purpose of applying mindfulness to our lives – the cultivation of genuine happiness.

Many of the greatest thinkers throughout history – from Greek philosophers such as Aristotle and Roman emperors like Marcus Aurelius, to psychologists such as William James and spiritual leaders including the Dalai Lama – have all commented that the pursuit of genuine happiness is the purpose of life. But where does happiness come from and how does mindfulness contribute to creating greater happiness?

ALWAYS LOOK ON THE BRIGHT SIDE OF LIFE – SPARTACUS

Interestingly, one of the biggest ideas that you'll find repeated in most self-help psychology books is the idea that events in our lives only affect us by the way we interpret them. According to these pop-psychology books, if we can alter our interpretations of the world, then we can also alter our experience of it. Sounds simple, doesn't it?

Actually, this idea has its origins in the early Stoicism of the third century BC, and later the Roman emperor Marcus Aurelius also expressed similar views. Aurelius suggested that, "If you are distressed by anything external, the pain is not due to the thing itself, but to your estimate of it; and this you have the power to revoke at any moment."[24] I'm not altogether sure, however, that slaves like Spartacus got the earlier memo!

In many ways, though, there is truth in this idea and it's not dissimilar to Buddha's observation that, "What we are today comes from our thoughts of yesterday, and our present thoughts build our life of tomorrow: our life is the creation of our mind." In the search for happiness, both the Stoics and Buddha agree that striving for external goods or trying to make the world conform to our wishes is always futile. Happiness can only be found within by breaking our emotional attachment to events and then by reframing them to decrease the distress they cause and increase our sense of wellbeing.

THE EMOTIONAL THERMOSTAT

You might have already suspected that the mindfulness tradition would suggest that happiness is the by-product of achieving an inner calm, rather than the result of acquiring external wealth and material achievements. Well, you were right. This is not to suggest, however, that all external pursuits are unimportant. There is nothing inherently anti-materialistic about mindfulness. And there's certainly nothing noble or romantic about poverty or experiencing emotional and physical pain.

Instead, the mindfulness tradition draws our attention to the fact that nothing outside of yourself possesses inherent qualities sufficient to guarantee your happiness. And this is a view that is supported by at least two big findings in psychology.

The first finding is that most external factors influence happiness much less than you might expect. Psychologist Ed Diener, recognized as the world's leading researcher on happiness, reports that after more than three decades, "Research on subjective wellbeing reveals that most life circumstances ... have only a small effect on happiness."[25]

The second finding relates to the first and offers some explanation for it. No matter how much we change the external landscape of our lives through the accumulation of objects or achievements, we remain susceptible to the law of diminishing returns, or what economists call "declining marginal utility".

Sure, life is generally better when we possess economic security, have meaningful work, enjoy good health and experience the love of friends and family. However, decades of research in psychology confirm that once our basic needs for security, comfort and independence are met, we recalibrate our expectations so that more and more of anything produces less and less satisfaction.

This experience is due, in part, to what psychologist and neuroscientist Richard Davidson refers to as our "set-point". Using EEG imaging, Davidson has been able to map particular activity in the brain that is correlated with positive emotions such as happiness. By correlating activity in the left prefrontal cortex of the brain with feelings of wellbeing, Davidson has found that each of us has a set-point for happiness that operates like an emotional thermostat. What's more, it appears to be genetically hardwired into us.

If these two big findings are correct, then we are all stuck on what psychologists have called the "hedonic treadmill". That is, no matter whether fortunate or unfortunate events occur in our lives, after a while we all have a tendency to gravitate once again toward our set-point for happiness.

MINDFULNESS, MONKS AND MOOD

Fortunately, there is hope. In his research, Davidson examined the brains of Tibetan Buddhist monks who reported attaining exceptionally high and sustainable levels of happiness. In these studies, monks who had undergone training in meditation were asked to meditate under controlled conditions, their heads wired with EEG electrodes. These monks achieved and maintained high levels of activity in the left prefrontal cortex – well above anything achieved by volunteer control subjects.

And although we may never have the opportunity (or the desire) to dedicate ourselves to years meditating in a mountain hermitage (let alone live the life of a celibate monk), the good news is, according to Davidson, that even brief regular meditation practice involving ten minutes a day can shift the set-point in the direction of greater wellbeing. Simply put, the more we meditate, the better we get at it and the happier we feel.

THE PSYCHOLOGY OF THE FOUR IMMEASURABLES

Not that long ago, I had the good fortune to have lunch with Matthieu Ricard, one of the monks who has worked with Davidson from the beginning. Ricard is described by *Time Magazine* as "the happiest person on earth," so I couldn't resist asking him for a few tips. He told me that "Looking for happiness selfishly is the best way there is to make yourself unhappy." Since the mindfulness tradition views everybody as interdependent and interconnected, our own happiness and unhappiness are closely tied up with the happiness and unhappiness of others. So, his advice: "Cultivate love and compassion for others; it's a win-win situation."

Ricard's advice is grounded squarely in the mindfulness tradition, which emphasizes that genuine happiness is cultivated through developing a good heart by practising the four attitudes of loving-kindness, compassion, joy and equanimity, or impartiality. These four attitudes (known as The Four Immeasurables) are pro-social in nature and designed to expand our sense of connection to others and guide us in our daily interactions.

From a psychological point of view, they operate on a principle known as reciprocal inhibition. The mind can only hold one thought or attitude at a time, so when we practise kindness or compassion regularly, we counteract negative emotions. The four attitudes therefore operate like antidotes to selfishness, anger, hatred or indifference, and create the conditions for greater happiness.

Ricard's advice is also completely in accord with four of the biggest and most robust findings to emerge from the happiness literature.

CULTIVATE RELATIONSHIPS

First, the strength and number of a person's relationships appears over and over again as the single most important predictor of happiness.[26] Good relationships make people happy, and happy people enjoy more and better relationships than unhappy people.[27] This implies that if you begin today to improve and cultivate your relationships, you will enjoy more positive emotions. These elevated feelings of happiness will also help you attract more and higher quality relationships, creating what psychologist Sonja Lyubomirsky refers to as an "upward spiral".[28]

PRACTISE KINDNESS

Second, Lyubomirsky and her colleagues at the University of California have conducted numerous experiments showing that increasing kind behaviors is an effective way to elevate happiness. In addition to contributing to other people's happiness, she suggests that being kind and generous leads to several personal benefits, such as developing a heightened sense of interdependence and cooperation, feeling advantaged and grateful, and gaining a new view of yourself as a altruistic and compassionate person.

EXPRESS GRATITUDE

Third, expressing gratitude is the ultimate approach to achieving happiness. Once again, according to Lyubomirsky, gratitude involves strategies such as looking at the bright side of a setback, thanking someone in your life, "counting your blessings", savoring moments, and not taking things for granted. It is a mindset that is present-oriented and involves a sense of wonder, thankfulness and appreciation for life. From a mindfulness perspective, it also includes taking pleasure in the happiness of others and wishing others wellbeing and success.

MINDFULNESS OF THE MUNDANE

Finally, findings from positive psychology confirm that those who open themselves to the beauty and excellence around them are more likely to find joy, meaning and profound connection in their lives.

It may appear immensely challenging to experience awe in response to mundane daily life, but it is an ability well worth cultivating. Many daily activities you take for granted contain opportunities to be grateful for the leisure and endowment life has given you.

SUMMARY

Throughout the day, deliberately and actively bring kindness into your actions, speech and thoughts. Try experiments in which you bring loving-kindness to someone for a specific period of time – perhaps a family member or a co-worker. Cultivate greater joy by finding genuine reasons to be grateful for the rich and diverse experiences that make up your life. Treat people kindly; remember, they're fighting a battle as well. Approach everyone with a non-judgmental, impartial attitude. Take renewed pleasure in the simple things, lighten up, and don't sweat the small stuff. Most importantly, make peace of mind your highest priority each day, and schedule time for the cultivation of your mind through mindfulness and meditation.

THE PRACTICE

✓ Make peace of mind your highest priority each day.

✓ Cultivate your relationships by paying regular attention to each person in your friendship network.

✓ Find creative ways to show kindness to people as often as you can.

✓ Adopt an optimistic perspective by looking for the opportunities to regroup and recommit to action after every setback.

✓ Take the time to thank someone in your life every day.

✓ Develop an attitude of gratitude and "count your blessings".

✓ Practice mindfulness of moments throughout the day, savoring the extraordinary experiences contained in even mundane moments so that you're not taking things for granted.

✓ Develop a mindset that is present-oriented and involves a sense of wonder, thankfulness and appreciation for life.

✓ Take pleasure in the happiness of others and wish others wellbeing and success.

PART FOUR

LIVING MINDFULLY

CHAPTER 15
MINDFULNESS AND STRESS MANAGEMENT

The greatest weapon against stress is our ability to choose one thought over another.

William James

It's not stress that kills us, it is our reaction to it.

Hans Selye, endocrinologist

It's not surprising to me that much of the current interest in mindfulness in the West has been generated due to the overwhelming body of evidence linking mindfulness practice to stress reduction and physical healing. As we saw in Chapter 5, a long list of scientific publications over the last 15 years have documented the effectiveness of mindfulness in treating medical conditions, many of which are now understood to be stress-related diseases.

Since the second half of the 20th century, stress has been identified as one of the most virulent causes of ill health in the Western industrialized economies. But this hasn't always been the case.

In 1925, a young medical student named Hans Selye was fascinated by something he observed while studying the science of diagnosis.

He noticed that many of the case studies he reviewed for diagnosis, although from a range of different illnesses, had many of the same symptoms. This phenomenon he would much later call a "syndrome of being sick". He could not have known that his observation would go on to have a profound impact on modern medical diagnosis.

At the time, Selye's observation was met with opposition, if not hostility, by his colleagues. The idea that many of the illnesses that brought people to the attention of physicians – such as high blood pressure, angina, digestive problems, rheumatism, and most nervous and mental disorders – were caused by a common set of diverse agents seemed improbable to the medical establishment at the time. Building on the work of psychologist Walter Cannon, Selye began to explore what happened to animals and people when they maintained a constant state of arousal. By 1946, he had sufficient evidence for his findings and coined a term that enabled him to convey his idea succinctly – "stress".

At least 50 years of research shows stress is generally bad for people, contributing to depression, anxiety disorders and heart disease. And many reports, including those from the World Health Organization, indicate that as the pace and complexity of modern life increases, we can expect to see a massive increase in stress-related disorders over the coming decade.

SPEED AND COMPLEXITY: THE GOOD, THE BAD AND THE UGLY

In the most recent book to document the speed and pace of change, entitled *The Great Acceleration*,[29] Robert Colvile builds a persuasive case that speeding up is one of the most significant modern social changes. While the book is generally positive and makes the point that speed can be a good thing – for example, we get more of what we want and we're better informed – Colvile makes it clear, however, that people often feel seriously troubled by this fast-moving environment. He quotes studies suggesting people are spending up to half their working days processing emails and that 94% of workers report that at some point they have felt "overwhelmed by information, to the point of incapacitation."

From a health and wellbeing point of view, the problem is that the speed and complexity of modern life causes the continuous activation of the hormonal response to danger, triggering the fight, flight or freeze response. Of course, the fight, flight or freeze response depends on our perceptions and thoughts. Whenever we think something or someone is a potential threat to us, we experience heightened arousal. Experiencing this stressful arousal on a regular basis can lead to psychological trauma and is thought to be a major contributor, either directly or indirectly, to coronary heart disease, cancer, lung ailments, accidental injury, cirrhosis of the liver and suicide – six of the leading causes of death in the West. No wonder why the research on the stress-reducing benefits of mindfulness has captured so much interest.

Of course, not all arousal is bad for us. Hard work and exercise are good for both our bodies and minds, and rising to meet adversity in life can have many beneficial effects, including building resilience. Selye tried to overcome this potential confusion by distinguishing between "good stress" and "bad stress." In Selye's view, good stress is anything that leads to a positive outcome, and bad stress is anything that leads to damaging consequences. Personally, I'm not altogether sure he succeeded in clearing up the confusion. By his definition, you don't know whether you have had good or bad stress until after the consequences – a heart attack, for example!

In my view, the better approach to understanding stress, as well as the potential benefits of mindfulness in reducing its damaging effects, is to understand the physiology of autonomic balance.

AUTONOMIC BALANCE – THE MASTER SWITCH

As we've discussed previously, the autonomic or involuntary nervous system has two divisions: on the one hand, the sympathetic branch prepares for emergencies; it increases heart rate and blood pressure, for example. This makes sense because in an emergency the critical function is to maintain blood flow to the brain and prepare the body for fight or flight. During an emergency, all other non-essential functions, such as digestion, are reduced.

On the other hand, the parasympathetic nervous system has precisely the opposite effect: it slows the heart rate and also lowers blood pressure. While reading these pages, your heart rate would be around 112 beats per minute instead of around 72 beats per minute if not for the parasympathetic system. These two systems are intended to alternate and work in balance, and when they do, we experience greater physical and emotional wellbeing.

The problem for many seriously busy people under stress and often in a continuous state of mild anxiety, is that the sympathetic system experiences constant stimulation. This can lead to a range of physical symptoms but, from a psychological point of view, it can leave us in a constant state of over-arousal or hyper-alertness, leading to emotional exhaustion.

IT'S RIGHT UNDER YOUR NOSE

Mindfulness practice can work to help soothe the body and calm the mind and bring about greater emotional balance through its impact on the autonomic nervous system. And the solution is literally right under your nose.

As we've seen, many approaches to mindfulness training focus on the breath. At the unconscious level, breathing is a bodily function that occurs automatically, thanks to the autonomic nervous system. It is also something that you can do voluntarily and, as a result, breath is a function through which you can influence the autonomic nervous system. In other words, by altering your breathing you can consciously address potential imbalances in the autonomic nervous system. And it's this imbalance that underlies many common physical disorders such as high blood pressure, as well as psychological disorders such as anxiety.

For example – and now this gets interesting – when we inhale, we directly stimulate the sympathetic nervous system, whereas when we exhale we directly stimulate the parasympathetic nervous system. It's possible, therefore, to influence your autonomic system directly by deliberately focusing on the ratio of inhalation to exhalation.

THE RELAXING MINDFUL BREATH TECHNIQUE

When clients I work with, either in the clinic or in a corporate context, tell me that they have problems related to anxiety or stress, I always encourage them to pay mindful attention to their breath. I then teach them a basic relaxation technique based on breath work. I can't tell you how many people over the years have told me how powerful and effective they find this technique for reducing anxiety and controlling stress.

The relaxing mindful breath technique that I describe for you here involves breathing in which you exhale twice as long as you inhale. It's actually a yoga technique and works to increase the activity of the parasympathetic system. In the short term, it's designed to provide you with an effective refuge from stress and anxiety. In the long term, it works to bring these two systems back into balance. This is a practice I use on a daily basis and recommend that you practice this at least twice a day. It's particularly useful to practice during periods of heightened arousal or stress to relax the body and calm the mind and restore clarity of focus.

To practice the relaxing mindful breath, use the exercise described in "The Practice" section to guide you, or download *The Relaxing Mindful Breath Technique* MP3 from the website for a more detailed guided meditation.

THE PRACTICE

The Relaxing Mindful Breath Technique
In this exercise, you inhale through your nose gently but deeply so that your abdomen expands. And, unlike the previous mindfulness breathing exercises, in this one you exhale through your mouth. Some traditions suggest that you place the tip of your tongue on the rigid tissue just above your front teeth and exhale around your tongue. Try this if it's comfortable.

You're going to first inhale through your nose, mindfully aware of your breath to a count of four. Then hold your breath for a count of seven. Then exhale through your mouth to a slow count of eight, relaxing as you do, mindfully aware of the breath all the way to the end of the exhalation

Remember to slow the rate of exhalation so that it's twice as long as the inhalation – a ratio of 2:1 Repeat that for a total of eight cycles, relaxing deeply with each out breath. I recommend that you never do more than eight cycles in one practice.

Once you've completed the sequence, simply breathe normally and observe how you feel; relaxed body, calm mind.

Of course, with practice once you've established a gentle rhythm, you can stop the mental counting and instead focus more mindfully on the smoothness and evenness of the breath flow, paying attention to what happens to your body and mind. Over time, you will find that practicing this technique regularly increases your resilience to stress and leads to a calmer and more peaceful mind. So I want to encourage you to make time each day – and particularly at night before going to sleep – to practice this technique and notice the changes that take place.

CHAPTER 16
MINDFULNESS AT WORK

Your work is to discover your work and then with all your heart give yourself to it.

Buddha

May your work be in keeping with your purpose.

Leonardo Da Vinci

According to Daniel Goleman, the primary task of leadership in any organization is to direct attention. Of course, he's right, but this is not easy! Managers have to deal with the increasing speed and complexity of leading in today's exciting, but frantic, information-driven work environments.

Workplaces have always been busy places, but the scale of information technology has massively accelerated the process of change, as well as accentuated the blurred lines between professional and personal life. How often do you check your e-mail or other productivity app? If you're like most people, the answer is continuously, even on weekends and holidays.

Organizations are under pressure to ensure that their people have the resources they need to manage the increasing personal demands that their professional roles make on them.

BELIEVE IN BETTER

Recently there has been widespread interest and enthusiastic media coverage of mindfulness in the workplace. High-profile global corporations such as Google, LinkedIn, Twitter and Sony, to name but a few, have all recently introduced mindfulness programmes.

The European media giant Sky, for example, is a stronghold of a workplace that combines speed with innovation. Just a few years ago, Sky was the maverick challenger to media establishments such as the BBC and ITV. Now the market leader in Europe, Sky thrives on a culture of critical thinking and innovation, and has a reputation of a demanding workplace culture. So when I was asked just two years ago to launch a leadership programme at Sky, based on mindfulness and emotional intelligence, I was surprised to find such universal enthusiasm for the programme.

MAKE PEACE OF MIND A PRIORITY

I remember well the impact of my opening comment at the launch of what is called the "Better Self" programme. I told the group, "The single most important skill you need in order to be able to lead well in the second half of your personal and professional life, is the ability to develop a peaceful mind." You could have heard a pin drop as participants realized the difficulty they had in calming their minds for more than just a few seconds at a time.

When you are under pressure and your mind is in a fog of stress, it's difficult to think clearly and impossible to generate innovative ideas. I'm convinced that the ability to maintain a peaceful mind in the face of relentless pressure is a critical skill in the formation of sound judgment and clear decision-making at work. Mindfulness is therefore an indispensable skill to lead well in any contemporary organization.

At Sky, their tagline, "Believe in Better" is not just a slogan, it's a credo and aligns well with the objectives of mindfulness. In the end, mindfulness is about being our best selves and achieving more of our potential. People who are clear minded, more focused and collaborative are also more productive and create better organizations.

Some months after the initial programme at Sky, one senior leader told me that the skill he'd learned to calm his mind and focus his attention was the "single most important personal and professional skill I've ever learned." When the mind is calm, we are able to think more clearly and make better decisions.

THE MYTH OF MULTITASKING

The context in which we work has changed radically in recent years. Workplaces have always been demanding, but people in business today must manage a massive increase in competing demands, accelerated timescales, and often cross-functional responsibilities, not to mention the avalanche of e-mails, phone calls, text messages and social media. The impact of this information overload has forced all of us to multitask.

The problem is that when you're processing an avalanche of information all at once, you retain less detail. We've all had the experience of being introduced to someone and five minutes later suffered the embarrassment of not being able to recall their name. This is because it's difficult to filter out what deserves your attention from what doesn't, and our mind moves on quickly to the next piece of information.

From a neurological perspective, multitasking is an illusion. It's actually not possible to focus attention on two things at the same time. In reality, your attention bounces from one task or issue to the next all day long. And according to a number of recent studies, this is why multitasking leads to fatigue and impairs decision-making, creativity and judgment.[30] At the very least, it tires the brain and leads to wandering minds, that, according to Dan Goleman, "may be the single biggest waster of attention in the workplace."[31]

WORK IN WATERTIGHT COMPARTMENTS

The key to managing your attention more effectively is to work in watertight compartments. Focus your attention on your immediate experience – such as the immediate task at hand – more deliberately before moving to the next project. This is particularly important when having a conversation with someone.

Many of us have a tendency to manage our relationships while multitasking. While we're involved in conversation, our minds can be somewhere else entirely, processing three or four tasks in quick succession. And we've all had the experience of speaking with someone who is so caught up in their own agenda that they fail to pay attention to us or are indifferent to our experience or point of view. This chronic distractibility diminishes the exchange of quality information, innovative thinking, empathy and ultimately trust. And ironically, the overall effect when trust is low is that the speed at which an organization performs slows down.

By contrast, there's an extensive range of recent research that provides a powerful business case for mindfulness in the workplace.

The data demonstrates significant positive impact on employee engagement, retention, productivity, innovation and leadership effectiveness. Certainly in my experience, while sometimes difficult to measure, the equally tangible benefits of mindfulness in the workplace include impressive improvements in the quality of interpersonal relationships and team dynamics.

MINDFULNESS – A POSTURE OF ATTENTION

The most obvious challenge to communication and building effective engagement in the workplace is simple inattention. Multitasking and external factors, such as pressured schedules, distract you from giving your full attention to someone. But the real obstacle to paying attention is internal – your busy mind. When you're fatigued or under pressure, you look for shortcuts, such as passing premature judgment, preparing your rebuttal, advising, or offering premature reassurance, rather than really listening.

Like all mindfulness practice, the first step in paying attention begins with becoming aware of your body so that you're giving your physical attention to another person. Consider developing a body posture of attention.

You've heard expressions such as, "They were on the edge of their seats" and "He gave them the cold shoulder". This suggests that when we are engaged with what's going on, we display a body posture that moves toward the stimulus. In other words, when you want to communicate that you are paying attention to someone, make the decision to turn toward the person you are speaking with and make appropriate eye contact.

Become mindful of your voice. The appropriate use of tone, volume and rate of your verbal responses can enhance effective attention. To demonstrate that you really are paying attention to another person, you can pause slightly when they stop speaking to see if they wish to continue.

These are the physical mechanics of paying attention, but what a person wants most of all from someone listening to them is psychological presence. Make a commitment to suspend your own agenda and judgment for a few moments, however important, and apply a mindful approach characterized by openness and curiosity. Give people your full attention.

MINDFUL MEETINGS

What is true for managing interpersonal communication is also true for managing meetings. The challenge of attending back-to-back meetings throughout the day is mental and emotional contamination. You arrive in one meeting while still processing the issues from the previous one. Once again, the key application of mindfulness is to let go of whatever preoccupied you prior to the meeting and give your full attention to the meeting you are currently in. This is not easy to do unless you've cultivated a strong and stable capacity to manage your attention in watertight compartments.

CONCLUSION

Mindfulness at work potentially leads to the creation of a calmer, more cohesive and innovative culture. People who are clear minded, more focused and collaborative make better decisions and are also more productive.

One of the most effective mindfulness practices to help you transition between meetings, or between projects for that matter, is to practice the *Three-Minute Breathing Space Meditation* briefly described in "The Practice" section on the next page or go to the website and download the full *Three-Minute Breathing Space Meditation* MP3 and follow the guided version. The breathing space is a mini meditation that operates like a bridge between the immediate demands of what you're dealing with and the longer, formal meditations.

Many people tell me that, along with the *Relaxing Mindful Breath Technique*, this is one of the most valuable practices they learn during the training programme. I suspect that this may be because it is both a helpful mechanism for working in watertight compartments, as well as providing mini-breaks from the relentless build-up of stress throughout the day.

That's the theory – now try a short meditation practice for yourself. You can begin by following the exercise described in "The Practice" section below or download the One-Minute Meditation MP3 from the website, www.themindfulnessbook.co.uk, and follow the guided version.

THE PRACTICE

Three-Minute Breathing Space Meditation
Essentially it's a quick and simple meditation involving three steps:

1. During the first step, you spend a minute becoming more aware of the issues preoccupying your attention.

2. The second step allows you to disengage yourself from these issues by radically narrowing your attention to your breath, particularly around the abdomen.

3. The third step involves broadening and opening your awareness to your immediate experience, where you have the opportunity to anchor your attention firmly in relation to the situation you are dealing with.

ADDITIONAL PRACTICES:

✓ Work in watertight compartments, prioritizing projects and moving systematically through them rather than between them.

✓ Give your full attention to the people you are engaged with.

✓ Practice the "Three-Minute Breathing Space Meditation" described above between meetings and at the end of the day before arriving home.

✓ Use the *Relaxing Mindful Breath Meditation* to avoid acting or speaking on impulse and to reduce the build-up of tension and anxiety.

✓ Never open your e-mails first thing in the morning before grabbing the opportunity to practice a few minutes of meditation to prepare yourself for the challenges of the day.

CHAPTER 17
MINDFULNESS
AND MANAGING
DIFFICULT EMOTIONS

If you wish to live a life free from sorrow, think of what is going to happen as if it had already happened.

Epictetus, Stoic philosopher

Life can be understood backwards, but must be lived forwards.

Søren Kierkegaard, philosopher and theologian

More than three decades ago, I remember reading a book that had a profound effect on my life and ultimately influenced my decision to become a psychologist. *The Road Less Travelled*,[32] written by psychiatrist M. Scott Peck, was memorable because it began with the unforgettable words "Life is difficult" and then went on to suggest that this is one of the greatest truths. Personally, I recognized the profound truth of this approach immediately because it stood in such sharp contrast to all my expectations about life.

I'd assumed that life shouldn't be difficult. And precisely because of this I had been complaining about the circumstances of my life, regularly bemoaning the things that had happened to me and the things that hadn't yet happened for me. Once I understood and accepted the truth of Peck's statement, to my surprise, almost instantly life felt less difficult.

LIFE IS SUFFERING

In describing life on these terms, Peck acknowledged that he owed this insight to Buddha's first teaching – that life is suffering. The mindfulness tradition is founded on this assumption but, as we saw in Chapters 10 and 12, it radically challenges Western psychology's diagnosis of the source of the problem. Happily, it also provides an incredibly effective series of approaches to dealing with our difficult emotions as well.

Most models of Western psychology quite naturally focus heavily on reducing the symptoms of distress. The mindfulness tradition, by contrast, isn't so much concerned with reducing symptoms, per se, as it is with changing the nature of our relationship to them.[33] So instead of suggesting a range of interventions designed to stop distressing thoughts or avoid difficult emotions directly, the mindfulness tradition prefers an approach designed to change the way we relate to our emotional difficulties. In the remainder of this chapter, I discuss five practical strategies for applying mindfulness to emotional problems.

STRATEGY 1 – TURN TOWARD DIFFICULTIES

To solve our problems effectively requires that we deal with the difficult and often distressing emotions they evoke. Yet, for many, this represents the biggest challenge. Because we fear the pain involved, almost all of us to some degree attempt to avoid problems. We try to deny them, ignore them or procrastinate, hoping that eventually they will fade away. According to mindfulness, this is a mistake.

Before moving into the study of cognitive psychology, I spent several years training in the psychoanalytical approach to psychology. As you may know, Freud used a number of Greek myths to help explain his theories of psychological development, including the myth of Oedipus, a mythical Greek king. Even if you don't know the details of the story, you're likely to remember Freud's shocking theory that it was about boys' secret desires to have sex with their mothers and kill their fathers.

It all started when Oedipus' dad, King Laius, consulted the Oracle at Delphi, who told him that if he and his wife ever had a son, the son would end up killing his father and marrying his mother. To avoid the prophecy, the king and queen gave baby Oedipus to one of their shepherds, telling him to leave the baby in the mountains to die. The shepherd couldn't bring himself to do this, so he handed Oedipus over to another shepherd, who then brought him to the King and Queen of Corinth, who adopted Oedipus and raised him as their own.

When Oedipus grew up, to his distress he found out about the prophecy. Obviously, Oedipus didn't know he was adopted, so he thought that the prophecy related to the mum and dad he knew. In order to avoid his fate he decided not to return to Corinth and, instead, headed toward the city of Thebes. On his way there, he met King Laius, his biological father. He got into a quarrel and ended up killing his father. The story gets more interesting and, as you might have guessed, he later ended up innocently marrying his real mother.

Of course, the moral of the story has little to do with Freud's "Oedipus complex". It's more often thought of as a story about how you can't escape your fate. However, I recently read an account by American Zen Buddhist and psychiatrist Barry Magid that offers a radically different interpretation and one consistent with the mindfulness tradition.

In an interview with Oliver Burkeman about his book, *Ending the Pursuit of Happiness*, Magid, says, "The quintessential point is that if you flee it, it will come back to bite you. The very thing from which you're in flight – well, it's the fleeing that brings on the problem."[34] In other words, according to Magid, struggling to avoid your demons is what gives them power. Psychological freedom and happiness are not found by avoiding our uncertainties, insecurities and fears but, instead, lie on the other side of turning toward them.

This is the first big insight from the mindfulness tradition. To approach your difficulties mindfully is to stop running away from the things that make you uncomfortable. Rather than striving hard to move away from your painful emotions or trying to fix your dysfunctional thoughts, mindfulness encourages you to watch these experiences dispassionately and learn to observe them as they are.

Admittedly, at first this can seem counterintuitive, especially when you consider that all of your biological drives have conditioned you to flee. But it makes perfect sense from a psychological point of view.

Take negative emotions such as anxiety or fear, for example. Both generate discomfort and strong urges to get rid of them or avoid them. Avoidance actually works well when you are confronted with physical threats, but fails hopelessly when dealing with psychological challenges like anxiety and fear. The more you attempt to avoid difficult thoughts and emotions through suppressing or avoiding them, more often than not this has the effect of amplifying them. And, as I've suggested previously, this typically often leaves you vulnerable to obsessive or compulsive behavior.

As you become aware of distressing or unpleasant emotions, the better strategy is to see if you can just allow these feelings to be as they are without moving away from them or trying to control them in any way. Simply observe them and see if you can label the feeling, such as "here's a feeling of anxiety" or "that's an angry feeling." At the very least, return your attention to your breathing to soothe the body and calm the mind if you become agitated.

STRATEGY 2 – LIVE IN THE NOW

If the first strategy entails turning more deliberately toward your experience, the second strategy involves bringing your focus completely into the present moment. One of the core tenants of mindfulness is "being in the moment" or "being fully present". This is important because, from a psychological perspective, all of our suffering tends to be created as our minds are caught up in issues either in the past, the future or both. We spend a lot of time ruminating about the past and anxious about the futures we imagine. The main focus of attention when we're being mindful is always the present moment. As Buddha put it, "The secret of health for both mind and body is not to mourn for the past, not to worry about the future, not to anticipate troubles, but to live in the present moment wisely and earnestly."

When you decide to focus more earnestly on the present moment, the noisy emotions from the past or future that either pull your mood down or fire your fear up can settle down.

STRATEGY 3 – ACCEPTANCE

The third strategy involves deciding to accept your experience as it is. Once you can create the psychological space through greater acceptance of your experience, you are able to reduce the potential negative gravitational pull of states such as depressed mood or anxiety that fog your mind.

By adopting a more accepting approach, you will likely discover that difficult emotions such as depressed mood, anxiety or fear are largely based on links to events in your past or imagined worries about your future, rather than an objective view of your current circumstances. Mindfulness opens up greater freedom to examine your experience dispassionately rather than being caught up in defending against it.

STRATEGY 4 – A NEW WAY OF SEEING

When you've turned toward your experience and accepted what you find, you can use the lenses of the "observing self" and "introspection" to recognize and begin to "name and explain" the thoughts and emotions you are experiencing. This has the effect of calming difficult emotions and helps prevent you from being overwhelmed by them. For example, there's a big difference between the experience of drowning in sad or angry feelings and recognizing that you are having sad or angry feelings and thoughts.

Rather than being caught up in ruminating about your experience or judging it, by employing your observing self you are able to adopt a level of detachment that operates like a disinterested spectator. This potentially opens up greater freedom of choice over your behavior.

STRATEGY 5 – LET IT GO

One final strategy involves the decision to let go of the tendency to be judgmental. Mindfulness proposes that the way to reduce your suffering is to reduce your degree of attachment to the objects and outcomes you desire. This entails learning to "let go" of your default tendency to hold judgments like; "I must have this" or "I can't stand that." This also involves letting go of your tendency to pass judgment on yourself: "I'm hopeless", "I'm guilty", "I'm inadequate" and so on. These judgments are often based on attachment to a false sense of your self and are not at all helpful to you or anyone who depends on you.

To live mindfully is to release the tight grip on the story about how something "should" or "shouldn't" be. Once you've loosened your grip on the stories and "self structures" that have rigidly defined you, you can pay closer attention to the values that guide your actions and make decisions accordingly.

SUMMARY

Dealing with difficult emotions mindfully, then, begins with turning toward your experience in the present moment, however difficult. When you take the lid off and have a look inside yourself, mindfulness encourages you to examine your experience dispassionately and accept what you find. Then examine your experience in light of your personal values. Treat yourself kindly, with compassion and integrity according to your cherished values, and act accordingly. This leads to greater psychological flexibility in your decision-making, and generates increased emotional freedom and a more peaceful mind.

To help you apply these practices in a formal way, go to the website, www.themindfulnessbook.co.uk, and download the *Mindfulness of Difficult Emotions Meditation* MP3 and follow the guided meditation.

THE PRACTICE

Mindfulness of Difficult Emotions Meditation
✓ Gently notice your temptation to move away from painful or unsettling thoughts, feelings and emotions.

✓ Instead, turn toward these thoughts and feelings and let them be without getting entangled in them through trying to analyse or "solve" them.

✓ Find a willingness to sit with them and look at them.

✓ If this is too difficult, focus on your body to put some space between your thoughts and the problem.

✓ Note your bodily sensation and remind yourself that you're not trying to change them, but to explore them with curiosity.

✓ Deepen your attitude of acceptance and openness by telling yourself that it's okay to feel this.

✓ Soften your body, relaxing more deeply with each out breath.

✓ If you are able, observe your thoughts and emotions and let them be.

✓ Treat yourself with kindness and compassion. However difficult the experience, embracing the things that cannot be changed and accepting the new reality takes time and courage.

✓ Through the difficulty, remember not to neglect the sweet spots of life still available to you – positive memories, beauty and innocence, but in particular, the opportunities to receive and show compassion that are all around you.

CHAPTER 18
ESTABLISHING YOUR MINDFULNESS PRACTICE

Real generosity toward the future consists in giving all to what is present.

Albert Camus, philosopher, author and journalist

The great thing about mindfulness as a skill is that it's the ultimate mobile technology. You can apply mindfulness anywhere at any time – whether dealing with challenges at work, playing with your child, managing difficult emotions or immersed in the daily domestic routines of life such as washing dishes, taking a shower or preparing a meal. Mindfulness leads to greater awareness of your experience, greater focus, less distraction, greater productivity and a more peaceful mind.

COVERING THE WORLD WITH LEATHER

The Tibetan Buddhist monk Yongey Mingyur Rinpoche relates an old Tibetan folktale that I find useful in highlighting how applying mindfulness works as a total approach to life. He describes a nomadic traveller who walked barefoot across the mountains and was constantly injured by the rugged terrain because he didn't have any shoes. During his travels, he would collect the skins of dead animals and spread them along the mountain paths, covering the stones and thorns. The problem was that this was hard work and slow going, as he could only cover several hundred square yards at a time. At last he realized that if he simply used a few small hides to make himself a pair of shoes, he could walk for thousands of miles with less effort and less pain. Simply by covering his feet with leather, he covered the entire earth with leather.

Mingyur explains that, in the same way, if you try to deal with each challenge or conflict, or each emotion and negative thought as it occurs, you're like the nomad trying to cover the world with leather. If, instead, you work at developing a more compassionate and peaceful mind, you can apply the same approach to dealing with most problems in your life.[35]

MANY TIMES, MANY MOMENTS

So if you ask me about when to practice mindfulness, the answer is, of course, "all the time". The problem with this answer is that, like New Year's resolutions, with all the good will in the world it takes time and practice to develop new skills and for these behaviors to become a natural expression of who you are.

Sometimes it's just not possible to make time for formal meditation practice every day. But it is possible to practice mindfulness informally for a few short minutes many times throughout the day.

Mindfulness is an approach that we bring to normal, even mundane activities such as washing the dishes, taking a shower, sitting in the car, walking up steps, drinking coffee, and yes, even breathing. Each of these activities provides an opportunity to quiet your mind for a few minutes and focus completely on the present experience, being aware of the sensory input, the sounds, smells and feelings associated with that experience.

For example, many people sip their morning coffee while reading the newspaper or catching up on the news. By taking the experience of drinking coffee for granted, they miss the richness and sensual pleasure of the experience. This is true of many activities we engage in on autopilot throughout the day.

Remember to adopt a more mindful approach while getting dressed, preparing food, washing your hands, walking to and from your home, and while engaging in conversation. This enables you to suck the marrow more completely from the experience – remember the chocolate meditation exercise from Chapter 1. In this way, any daily activity represents an opportunity to practice mindfulness.

ESTABLISH AN INTENTION – SET GOALS

The key here is intention. When attempting to bring mindfulness into your life, it can be helpful to be very intentional and set some goals. This takes us back to our initial understanding of mindfulness from the ancient Indian word *Sati*, which means to remember. Mindfulness is fundamentally about remembering to remember the present moment.

In the initial phase of developing mindfulness, it can be very helpful to set yourself a specific number of times that you intend to remember the present moment deliberately during the day. Then find an easy way to keep a record of your progress, as this will help you stay on track. Once you're comfortable with 20 short one-minute practices, you can gradually increase the number. In this way, you establish mindfulness through short, informal, present-moment practices. This not only makes each of your experiences more interesting, but also reinvests each experience with greater potential to contribute to your happiness. Finally, these short mindful practices will also make it much easier for you to settle when you sit down for longer, more formal meditation practice.

ESTABLISH YOUR MIND GYM SCHEDULE

To cultivate mindfulness, it's a good idea to set aside some time to practice more formal meditation for a few minutes every day. Meditation is like a mental gym for your mind. Scheduling formal training sessions develops the core strength necessary for sustained mindfulness practice.

If it's practical, make it a habit to rise as early as you can and set aside time for meditation at the start of each day. A lot of people find the first few minutes of each day the best time to practise. This is because it's generally easier to settle the mind before it becomes agitated by the concerns of the day. Of course, this assumes that you've broken the habit of checking your e-mails as you get out of bed! Others prefer the end of the day, before going to sleep, as a way of settling the mind. These two periods – just after waking and before sleeping – can be important because you are potentially in a more receptive frame of mind.

Personally, I prefer to practice at both ends of the day and, whenever I can, I make it a practice of going to bed slightly earlier than I need to. Not only does this create the space for a few minutes of practice before going to sleep, but it also allows me to be more of an early riser than when I was younger.

How you start the day, in particular, will have a significant impact on how you live the day. So I recommend taking a few minutes for practice at the beginning of each day.

THE BIG DISTRACTION – PROCRASTINATION

Once you begin to experience the benefits of mindfulness and meditation, chances are you'll be motivated to practice regularly. Yet, take it from me, it won't be long before you "fall off the wagon". Life has a habit of getting in the way of some of our best intentions. Before long you'll probably start putting off your practice until a more convenient time – and the rationalizations start to come thick and fast. Procrastination is quite literally the thief of time, especially of the present moment. And the bad news is, most anti-procrastination advice doesn't work, or at least not for very long.

The problem with most motivational strategies is that they are really all about trying to change how you feel about doing stuff. They assume that we put things off because we're not in the mood, and the mistaken belief that if we can change our mood then we can achieve our goals. Accordingly, they tend to focus on how to get us in the mood for getting things done.

Of course, sometimes feeling motivated can help. But this is particularly challenging for establishing a meditation practice because we keep ourselves busy "thinking" and "doing" for a reason – usually to manage anxiety. Remember Blaise Pascal's startling observation that I noted in the Introduction: "All of man's miseries stem from his inability to sit alone in a room." The act of sitting and quieting the mind is, at least initially, quite challenging.

DEALING WITH DISTRACTION – THE ZEIGARNIK EFFECT

In my view, the best advice for overcoming procrastination comes from William James. In the face of conventional wisdom, James believed that it was actually easier to act your way into a new kind of thinking and feeling than it was to think or feel yourself into a new way of acting. He described the "act as if" principle – a kind of early 20th century view of "Just do it".

According to James, if you want a quality such as passion, you should "act as if" you already have it. The impact that this will have in changing how other people see you and treat you will, in turn, help you feel differently. In other words, don't wait to get in the mood to meditate, just do it. Over time you'll find the experience itself so rewarding that the motivation will take care of itself. James' advice is supported by something psychologists call the "Zeigarnik Effect".

Back in the 1920s, Russian psychologist Bluma Zeigarnik realized that most people, once they've started something, dislike leaving the task unfinished. In some recent research, participants were asked to work on solving complex puzzles. After a few minutes, they were interrupted before they could get all the pieces together and asked to stop working. Ninety per cent of interrupted participants kept working on their puzzles.

What the Zeigarnik Effect teaches us is that the best approach for dealing with procrastination is starting somewhere, anywhere. When people manage to start something, they're actually more inclined to finish it. Seems simple, but the concept has been proven over and over for decades. So the idea is to "act as if" you meditate regularly.

But there is one other important factor to keep in mind. It doesn't work so well when you think the task is daunting. So rather than attempting 30-minute meditation sessions, begin with short sessions of 5 to 6 minutes each day and build from there.

THE PRACTICE

✓ Practice mindfulness during mundane activities such as washing the dishes, taking a shower, sitting in the car, walking up steps, or drinking a cup of coffee.

✓ Quiet your mind for a few minutes and focus completely on the present experience, being aware of the sensory input, the sounds, smells, and feelings associated with that experience.

✓ Establish your intention to be mindful throughout the day and set a specific number of times you intend to practice one-minute mindful moments. Gradually increase the number.

✓ Set aside a few minutes for formal meditation practice at the beginning or end of the day. Start with six-minute sessions.

✓ Remember the Zeigarnik Effect – just do it!

CHAPTER 19
SEVEN TIPS FOR BECOMING MORE MINDFUL

Of all ridiculous things, the most ridiculous seems to me to be busy – to be a man who is hurried about his food and his work.

Søren Kierkegaard

When you were young, the chances are you were told overtly, or at least inadvertently, that achieving anything worthwhile "is all about being more disciplined." To be honest, I've never been a big believer in discipline. Don't get me wrong; I realize it takes a lot of hard work and dedication to achieve excellence in any field of endeavor. But once we're adults, personally I'm not convinced that discipline remains the key to making fundamental changes in our lives. Discipline is really a push strategy.

Sure, strong will and discipline push us to excel, but, like exceptional performance, we make real changes in our lives when we're pulled forward by the things we really want to do. I'm convinced that the things we do best we do because we are compelled to do them. It's a pull strategy.

HABITS OF THE HEART

Every day we act with discipline about certain things that are important to us or that we enjoy, except it doesn't feel like discipline because our actions have become habits. After a while, new habits develop neurological connections and new behaviors become embedded like a brain tattoo.

In other words, you achieve best practice when two forces combine – when your values are engaged and when you practise behaviors that are an expression of those values until they become habits of the heart. Nowhere is this truer than when establishing the habit of mindfulness. Over the years, I've found a number of additional practices that have contributed to my becoming more mindful. I try to practise them every day and recommend them to you as a set of guideposts to becoming more mindful.

SEVEN PRACTICES FOR LIVING MINDFULLY

1. THE PRACTICE OF SOLITUDE

For most of us, our lives are filled with noise and activities from the moment we open our eyes. We wake up and check our e-mails, eat our breakfast while catching up on the news of the day or organizing the kids, and listen to the radio as we drive our cars. We arrive at work and pinball from meeting to meeting or activity to activity against the background of relentless information technology demanding our attention.

Taking a few moments each day for solitude and quiet allows your mind to settle. From a neurological point of view, as your mind settles and you tune in to your awareness, the speed of the electrical impulses generated by your brainwaves slows. This moves your mind into a mild altered state of consciousness. In this state, you are more likely to experience creative inspiration or intuitive insight that comes from accessing your multiple intelligences.

Ideally, find a quiet space either at home or in nature where you can spend a few minutes allowing your mind to settle. Practising a few minutes of mindfulness of the body can be a great way to move out of the narrative mode and into a more relaxed state of mind and body.

2. THE PRACTICE OF MEDITATION

Beyond finding moments of solitude each day, it's a good idea to set aside regular time to practise meditation for a short period every day. How you start the day, in particular, will have a significant impact on how you live the day. As you know, I like to start each day in the mind gym of meditation to strengthen and balance my mind. Taking a few minutes for practice at the beginning of each day has the effect of preparing your mind for the day ahead. Meditation balances and clarifies the mind so that you can apply it effectively to the challenges of the day ahead.

3. THE PRACTICE OF MOVEMENT

We know that regular physical exercise leads to a range of health benefits, including improved mood and enhanced emotional well-being. Personally, I have found regular exercise to be indispensible for generating and renewing my physical and emotional energy, as well as for maintaining emotional balance.

You don't have to be a jock or an elite athlete to make exercise a regular part of your life. Many research studies examining the impact of exercise on emotional wellbeing have used walking or jogging programs, but some research finds nonaerobic exercise such as strength and flexibility training, as well as yoga, to be effective too.

In addition to the physical and emotional benefits of walking, walking can also be used as a formal meditation practice. This involves walking while concentrating closely on every step you take. Walking also provides an excellent opportunity for a more informal practice of mindfulness through maintaining open awareness. After a while, you can expand your awareness to your environment and allow your attention to flow across the sights, sounds and smells around you. Try a walking meditation practice for yourself by downloading the *Walking Meditation* MP3 and follow the guided version.

4. THE PRACTICE OF CONNECTING WITH NATURE

Of course, if your preferred form of exercise involves walking or running, chances are you do this in a park, at the beach or some other place in nature. We are part of the natural order and cannot enjoy optimum physical or emotional wellbeing if we have too little contact with it. During a busy week, the simple act of walking or sitting in a park and observing the environment around me has the effect of quieting my mind and evoking a sense of peace. Connecting with nature is a grounding experience, during which my priorities become clearer. Again, this provides a natural support for mindfulness and generates the ideal conditions for creative thought.

5. THE PRACTICE OF KINDNESS AND COMPASSION

At the end of his life, the writer, novelist and philosopher Aldous Huxley summed up one of the most essential lessons he'd learned during his life: "Let us be kinder to one another." As we've seen, the regular practice of mindfulness involves approaching our experience non-judgmentally, with an attitude of openness and curiosity. This inevitably generates a more compassionate and understanding approach toward others and ourselves.

Psychologist Dacher Keltner is convinced that we are "Born to be good" and that practicing kindness toward others is written into our DNA. However, we typically only extend this kindness to those within our circle of care. Practising mindfulness quite naturally extends our circle of care. And working to improve the lives of others, through acts of generosity and kindness, leads to a richer and more meaningful life.

6. THE PRACTICE OF CLEAN AND LEAN

I was fortunate to grow up in an environment where there was always food on the table. My parents worked hard to ensure that we never went without and for that I'm grateful. Today, however, we understand so much more about the importance of diet and the role it plays in our health and wellbeing. An inadequate diet has a serious detrimental effect not only on your body, but also on your mental health. It negatively affects your mood and reduces the clarity of your mind.

The Australian trainer and nutritionist James Druigan coined the term "clean and lean"[36] to refer to his philosophy of only eating food that nourishes the body and mind. James has a simple and distinctive ethos when it comes to nutrition: "Be kind to yourself." He advocates avoiding refined, processed and manufactured food. Instead, eat only clean or whole foods with ingredients that come from nature, free of pesticides, toxins and refined sugars. This practice can significantly reduce the destructive pressures of modern living.

Recent research has also suggested that supplementing your diet with omega-3 fatty acids, particularly from fish oils, and vitamin D can play a major role in elevating your emotional set point. This is a practice I have found to be enormously beneficial in helping to manage my mood on a daily basis.

Of course, being mindful of what you eat is the first step. Paying attention to how you eat – by eating more slowly and mindfully – enables you to connect with your senses and enjoy greater appreciation of the vivid and intense flavors of the experience.

7. THE PRACTICE OF GRATITUDE

As I study the mindfulness tradition, I'm constantly reminded to be grateful for the extraordinary opportunities that are available to me. This is not always easy, especially when dealing with life's disappointments and setbacks. During these times, it's easy to lose perspective and forget what you have to be grateful for. This can be particularly true when you compare your life to others who are more prosperous, better educated or who appear to be living charmed lives.

An 8th century Buddhist monk, Shantideva, offers an antidote to feelings of envy and resentment, and reminds us that we have both "leisure and endowment". By this he means each of us has a combination of freedom, time, intelligence and education that are rare gifts in the scheme of things. The very fact that you have "endowments", such as the financial means to buy this book, and the intelligence and education to consider the ideas discussed in it, and the leisure to read it, already places you among a small group of the world's most privileged people. Simply being mindful of these gifts on a daily basis represents a "perfect opportunity" to live an extraordinary life if you will take advantage of them.

Of course, we are fortunate, but how often do we forget to be grateful for the many small but important things in our lives. By its very nature, practising gratitude reinforces mindfulness because it leads you to focus on the present moment. It involves the cultivation of a mindset that is increasingly appreciative of your life as it is today and all that has contributed to it.

Psychologists refer to the deliberate practice of asking yourself what you have to be thankful for as "appreciative enquiry". It's a mindset that is present-moment-oriented and involves a sense of wonder, thankfulness, curiosity, openness and appreciation for life. Practise regularly!

CHAPTER 20
CONCLUSION:
THE BEGINNER'S MIND

The real voyage of discovery consists not in seeking out new land-scapes, but in having new eyes.

Attributed to **Marcel Proust**, 1871-1922

There are only two ways to live your life. One is as though nothing is a miracle. The other is as though everything is a miracle.

Albert Einstein

At the start of this book, I shared William James' startling observation that the ability to focus our minds by bringing our attention back to the present moment was the indispensable skill that enabled people to take control of their lives and achieve their potential. And more than a century later, his simple observation has had a profoundly positive impact on the lives of millions of people as they have discovered the practice of mindfulness.

Even though James knew little of the ancient practice we call mindfulness, he did understand the revolutionary implications of having the ability to alter our state of mind. He went on to suggest: "The greatest discovery of my generation is that human beings can alter their lives by altering their attitude of mind ... If you change your mind, you can change your life." This is the real promise of mindfulness: the cultivation of a new mindset.

To conclude, I'd like to offer you one final insight about how to approach your mindfulness practice that, personally, I have found to be very powerful.

THE BEGINNER'S MIND

In the beginning, learning any new skill takes time and patience, and this is true of mindfulness. Throughout this book I have described mindfulness in terms of a set of psychological skills acquired through practice to achieve a more peaceful mind. This is simply the beginning. Perhaps the real value of mindfulness is found in its capacity to expand our consciousness, to see new possibilities in the world around us. So the best advice I can give you is to approach your practice with a "beginner's mind".

The idea of the "beginner's mind" was one of the favorite phrases of Shunryu Suzuki Roshi, who brought Zen meditation from Japan to America in the 1960s. According to him, "In the beginner's mind there are many possibilities, but in the expert's mind there are few."[37] Of course, the more we learn, the more we realize the extent of our ignorance.

As a psychologist, when I think of the beginner's mind I think of the experience of a child, full of curiosity, wonder and amazement. Behind the idea of a beginner's mind there is a perception that we must recapture elements of a child's mind if we are to live authentically and mindfully.

CURIOSITY AND WONDER

Children come into the world with a natural sense of curiosity and wonder. When they discover something new, they have no label for this particular "thing", and no past or present links with it. This means they don't approach their experience with a fixed point of view or prior judgment. They see the object with fresh, innocent eyes, just asking, "What is it?" "What does this mean?"

IMMEDIACY AND THE PRESENT MOMENT

Of course, I'm not suggesting that mindfulness encourages us to return to the state of innocence represented by the mind of a child. That would be dangerous. When I speak of the innocence of a child, it is this quality of immediacy, their ability to be spontaneously in the present moment that is so characteristic. The primary mode of time in which the child lives is the now.

Furthermore, children approach their experiences with so few expectations. This allows them to be surprised and delighted by the novelty and beauty in each moment.

OPENNESS AND CURIOSITY

The celebrated child psychologist Jean Piaget suggested that children do not tend to see the world as operating according to laws and live in a world where anything is possible. Their world is only limited by their imagination. Because of this, they don't tend to get bored with things that are familiar. It's this openness and curiosity, and lack of predictability that allows a child to enjoy the same game or song over and over again.

MASTERY ACTION AND WONDER

Finally, the developing world of the child is not primarily one of thinking, but of experience and action. New situations present a challenge to be mastered through experience. Psychologist and philosopher Sam Keen has observed that some people assume that as a child develops reason and the ability to think, that the child loses the sense of wonder, but according to Keen, this is not true. As the child develops the ability to reason, this only fuels the excitement of discovering new things.[38]

Mindfulness does not ask us to abandon thinking; it is not anti-intellectual. It simply asks us to consider another way of knowing that enhances the mind's potential. Perhaps this is best illustrated with a simple historical anecdote.[39]

We all remember the story of Archimedes and his bath. What you may not know is that Archimedes was a mathematician, physicist, engineer and inventor. In fact, some historians consider him the finest mathematician who ever lived, so definitely no slouch. The backstory involves King Hiero II, who had supplied pure gold to a goldsmith to create his personal crown. The only problem was that the king didn't trust the goldsmith, so he asked Archimedes to determine whether or not the potentially dishonest goldsmith had substituted some silver. Of course, Archimedes had to solve the problem without damaging the crown in anyway – not easy!

Try as he may, he could not find a way to solve this intractable problem. He'd basically given up thinking about the problem and decided instead to take a bath. Obviously he'd done this many times before, but as he slipped into the water this time, he noticed that the level of the water in the tub rose as he got in. He realized immediately that the submerged crown would displace an amount of water equal to its own volume. Archimedes was so excited by his discovery that he ran out into the streets naked, shouting Eureka – meaning "I found it!"

This is a superb illustration of what happens to the mind and our intelligence when we make time for a little mindfulness. As we move more fully into the immediacy of our present experience and out of the narrative mode, and bring a relaxed awareness, even curiosity to the familiar, we create the conditions for the mind in which genuine creativity and discovery can occur.

As the American writer Henry David Thoreau said: "What lies behind us and what lies before us are small matters compared to what lies within us. And when we bring this out into the open, miracles happen." I'm convinced that mindfulness is a powerful tool for cultivating the potential within you. It is my sincere hope that you find this short introduction a valuable guide to practising mindfulness – and that it helps you to live a more peaceful, productive and creative life.

NOTES AND
FURTHER READING

1. William James, *The Principles of Psychology* (New York: Dover Publications, 1890/1958).

2. Some contemporary approaches to psychotherapy, such as, 'Acceptance and Commitment Therapy' (ACT) adopt these insights and incorporate mindfulness as a psychological intervention. See Russ Harris, *The Happiness Trap: Stop Struggling and Start Living*. Wollombi, NSW, Australia: Exisle Publishing , 2006.

3. Jon Kabat-Zinn, *Wherever You Go, There You Are: Mindfulness Meditation for Everyday Life*, New York, Hyperion, 1994.

4. B Alan Wallace, *Minding Closely: The Four Applications of Mindfulness*, New York: Snow Lion Publications, 2011.

5. Goldin, P. & Gross, J. "Effects of Mindfulness-Based Stress Reduction (MBSR) on Emotion Regulation in Social Anxiety Disorder," *Emotion*, 10, 1. (2010): 83-91.

6. Davidson RJ, Kabat-Zinn J, Schumacher J, Rosenkranz M, Muller D, Santorelli SF, Urbanowski F, Harrington A, Bonus K, Sheridan JF. "Alterations in Brain and Immune Function Produced by Mindfulness Meditation," *Psychosomatic Medicine*, Jul-Aug; 65(4) (2003): 564-70.

7. Chiesa A, Serretti A. "Mindfulness-Based Stress Reduction for Stress Management in Healthy People: A Review and Meta-Analysis. *The Journal of Alternative and Complementary Medicine*, 15 (5) (2009): 593-600.

8. Hofmann, S. G., Sawyer, A. T., Witt, A. A., & Oh, D. "The Effect of Mindfulness-Based Therapy on Anxiety and Depression: A Meta-Analytic Review," *Journal of Consulting and Clinical Psychology*, 78, 2 (2010): 169-183.

9. Khoury B, Lecomte T, Fortin G, Masse M, Therien P, Bouchard V, et al. "Mindfulness-Based Therapy: A Comprehensive Meta-Analysis," *Clinical Psychology Review*; 33 (2013): 763-771.

10. Keng SL, Smoski MJ, Robins CJ. "Effects of Mindfulness on Psychological Health: A Review of Empirical Studies," *Clinical Psychology Review*, 31(6) (2011): 1041-1056.

11. Jha AP, Stanley EA, Kiyonaga A, Wong L, Gelfand L. "Examining the Protective Effects of Mindfulness Training on Working Memory and Affective Experience," *Emotion*, 10(1) (2010): 54–64.

Zeidan F, Johnson SK, Diamond BJ, David Z, Goolkasian P. "Mindfulness Meditation Improves Cognition: Evidence of Brief Mental Training," *Consciousness and Cognition*, 19(2) (2010): 597-605.

Mrazek MD, Franklin MS, Phillips DT, Baird B, Schoole JW. "Mindfulness Training Improves Working Memory Capacity and GRE Performance While Reducing Mind Wandering," *Psychological Science*, 24(5) (2013): 776-781.

12. Levy, D., Wobbrock, J., Kaszniak, A. & Ostergren, M. "The Effects of Mindfulness Meditation Training on Multitasking in a High-Stress Information Environment," *Proceedings of Graphics Interface*, (2012): 45-52.

13. Zeidan F, Johnson SK, Diamond BJ, David Z, Goolkasian P. "Mindfulness Meditation Improves Cognition: Evidence of Brief Mental Training," *Consciousness and Cognition*, 19(2) (2010): 597-605.

Mrazek MD, Franklin MS, Phillips DT, Baird B, Schoole JW. "Mindfulness Training Improves Working Memory Capacity and GRE Performance While Reducing Mind Wandering," *Psychological Science*, 24(5) (2013): 76-781.

14. B Alan Wallace, *Minding Closely: The Four Applications of Mindfulness*, New York: Snow Lion Publications, 2011.

15. Steven C. Hayes with Spencer Smith, *Get Out of Your Mind and Into Your Life: The New Acceptance and Commitment Therapy*, New York: MJF Books, 2005.

16. B Alan Wallace, *Minding Closely: The Four Applications of Mindfulness*, New York: Snow Lion Publications, 2011.

17. Martyn Newman, *Emotional Capitalists: The Ultimate Guide for Building Emotional Intelligence for Leaders*, London: RocheMartin. 2014. (First published by John Wiley & Sons.

18. Michel de Montaigne, *The Complete Essays* (Ed. & Trans., M. A. Screech), London: Penguin. 1991/1588.

19. Rick Hanson and Richard Mendius, *Buddha's Brain: The Practical Neuroscience of Happiness, Love & Wisdom*, Oakland: New Harbinger. (2009)

20. Peter Salovey and John D. Mayer, "Emotional Intelligence," *Imagination, Cognition, and Personality 9*, no 3 (1990): 185-211.

21. Newman, M., Purse, J., Smith, K., & Broderick, J. "Assessing Emotional Intelligence in Leaders and Organizations: Reliability and Validity of the Emotional Capital Report (ECR)," *The Australasian Journal of Organisational Psychology*, Volume 8, January 2015.

22. D. Goleman, *Focus: The Hidden Driver of Excellence*, (New York: HarperCollins), 2013, p. 62.

23. D. Goleman, *Focus: The Hidden Driver of Excellence*, (New York: HarperCollins), 2013, p. 78.

24. Marcus Aurelius, *Meditations* (Trans. Martin Hammond), London: Penguin, 2006.

25. Ed Diener and Rober Biswas-Diener, *Happiness: Unlicking the Mysteries of Psychological Wealth* (Malden, MA: Blackwell: 2008), p. 10.

26. Martin Seligman, *Authentic Happiness*. (New York: Free Press, 2002).

27. Lyubomirsky, S., King, L., & Diener, E. "The Benefits of Frequent Positive Affects: Does Happiness Lead to Success? *Psychological Bulletin Vol. 131, No. 6, 803–855. 2005.*Jonathan Haight, *The Happiness Hypthesis: Putting Ancient Wisdom and Philosophy to the Test of Modern Science*, (London: Arrow Books, 2006).

28. Sonia Lyubomirsky, "The How of Happiness: A Practical Guide to Getting the Life You Want," *Sphere*, p. 139.

29. Robert Colvile, *The Great Acceleration: How the World is Getting Faster, Faster* (London: Bloomsbury, 2016).

30. According to Derek Dean and Caroline Webb in their McKinsey & Company report, multitasking actually "makes human beings less productive, less creative, and less able to make good decisions," *McKinsey Quarterly*, January, 2012.

31. Dan Goleman, *Focus: The Hidden Driver of Excellence*, (New York: HarperCollins, 2013), p. 202.

32. M. Scott Peck, *The Road Less Travelled*, London: Arrow Books. 1990.

33. Note: This is also an approach advocated by a number of contemporary models of cognitive behavioral psychology, such as Dialectical Behavior Therapy and Acceptance and Commitment Therapy (ACT).

34. Oliver Burkeman, *The Antidote: Happiness for People Who Can't Stand Positive Thinking* (Edinburgh: Canongate, 2012), p. 56.

35. Yongey Mingyur Rinpoche, *The Joy of Living: Unlocking the Secret & Science of Happiness*. (New York: Three Rivers, 2007), p. 188.

36. James Duigan, *Clean and Lean for Life: The Cook Book*, London: Kyle Books. 2015.

37. Shunryu Suzuki-roshi, *Zen Mind, Beginner's Mind* (Ed. Trudy Dixon) Boston: Shambala, 2005.

38. American philosopher Sam Keen discusses these themes in philosophical and psychological detail in his book, *Apology for Wonder*, (New York: HarperCollins), 1980.

39. Richard Gilprin. *Mindfulness for Black Dogs & Blue Days: Finding a Path Through Depression*. Lewes, UK: Leaping Hare Press, 2012.

LIST OF AUDIO FILES

Available at www.themindfulnessbook.co.uk

1. *Introduction to the Mindfulness Audio Series* MP3/MP4
2. *The Chocolate Meditation* MP3
3. *One-Minute Meditation* MP3
4 *Mindfulness of Breathing Meditation – Short Practice* MP3
5. *Mindfulness of Breathing Meditation – Extended Practice* MP3
6. *Nine-Cycle Breathing Meditation* MP3
7. *The Body Scan Meditation* MP3
8. *Mindfulness of Thoughts and Feelings Meditation* MP3
9. *The Relaxing Mindful Breath Technique* MP3
10. *Three-Minute Breathing Space Meditation* MP3
11. *Mindfulness of Difficult Emotions Meditation* MP3
12. *Walking Meditation* MP3

ABOUT THE AUTHOR

Martyn Newman, PhD, DPsych, is a clinical psychologist with an international reputation as an expert in emotional intelligence (EQ) and mindfulness.

Martyn is a qualified mindfulness teacher and a graduate of the "Cultivating Emotional Balance Teacher Training" programme endorsed by the Dalai Lama and taught by Dr Paul Ekman and Dr B. Alan Wallace. He has extensive experience teaching leadership development and mindfulness programmes to senior executives at corporations such as Sky, ExxonMobil, Boeing and SingTel, among many others.

He is author of the best-selling book *Emotional Capitalists – The Ultimate Guide to Developing Emotional Intelligence for Leaders* and co-author of the *Emotional Capital Report*™ – the global benchmark for measuring emotional intelligence and leadership performance.

Martyn has held academic posts as senior lecturer in the department of psychology at the University of East London, and the school of psychology, ACU National. He is currently Visiting Fellow for Leadership and Emotional Intelligence at Sheffield Business School, Sheffield Hallam University, and an instructor in mindfulness with the MBA program at Sydney University.

Martyn received his PhD from the University of Sydney and holds an MA from GTU at the University of California, Berkeley; a Masters of psychology from Monash University Melbourne; and a Doctor of Psychology from La Trobe University, Melbourne.

FOLLOW MARTYN on twitter.com/MartynNewman.

**CONTACT MARTYN FOR ADVICE,
TRAINING OR SPEAKING OPPORTUNITIES:**
www.martynnewman.com